Evaluation of Reflective Vest Options

National Institute of Justice (NIJ), Aaron
Nisenson, Bruce Kubu, Ashley Carney

The author(s) shown below used Federal funds provided by the U.S. Department of Justice and prepared the following final report:

Document Title: Development of an Integrated Workflow from Laboratory Processing to Report Generation for mtDNA Haplotype Analysis

Author: Rhonda K. Roby, Ph.D., M.P.H.; Nicole R. Phillips, M.S.; Jennifer L. Thomas, M.S.; Marc Sprouse; Pam Curtis, M.S.

Document No.: 234292

Date Received: April 2011

Award Number: 2008-DN-BX-K192

FY 2008 Forensic DNA Unit Efficiency Improvement

The University of North Texas Health Science Center

Department of Forensic & Investigative Genetics

Project Duration: October 1, 2008 to December 31, 2010

Award Number: NIJ Cooperative Agreement 2008-DNA-BX-K192

Authors: **Rhonda K. Roby, PhD, MPH, Principal Investigator**; Nicole R. Phillips, MS; Jennifer L. Thomas, MS; Marc Sprouse; and Pam Curtis, MS

Scientific Team: **Rhonda K. Roby, PhD, MPH, Principal Investigator**; Israel Escobedo, MS; Suzanne D. Gonzalez, PhD; Nicole R. Phillips, MS; Marc Sprouse ; Jennifer L. Thomas, MS

Support Staff: Linda LaRose, MT (ASCP) and Hector Saenz, MT (ASCP)

Abstract

The University of North Texas Health Science Center (UNTHSC) maintains a full service forensic laboratory that is accredited under the requirements of ISO 17025 (International Organization for Standardization, 2005) and the DNA National Standards for DNA Analysis by the Forensic Quality Services - International Division (Federal Bureau of Investigation, 2009). The forensic laboratory consists of two divisions, the Laboratory of Forensic Anthropology and the Laboratory of Molecular Identification, and provides testing to law enforcement agencies nationally and internationally. The Laboratory for Molecular Identification is a full service laboratory with forensic DNA testing services, which include both STR (short tandem repeat) and mtDNA (mitochondrial DNA) testing, and a Field Testing Division (FTD), which has been involved with the development and testing of several procedures and commercial kits currently used in forensic casework and databasing laboratories.

The UNTHSC has identified several steps in the analysis of mtDNA for reference samples that can significantly reduce labor in both the laboratory and in data review, reduce the reagent costs, and reduce the overall analytical time. A reduction in labor, reagents, and processing time will improve efficiency and increase the overall capacity of mtDNA processing by the laboratory. The areas of improvement addressed in this project include chemistry, software development and enhancements, and robotics.

For chemistry improvements, the performance of the following were evaluated: a real-time quantitative PCR assay; a single amplicon which covers the entire control region of the mitochondrial genome (mtGenome); a reduced amount of ExoSAP-IT®; BigDye® Terminator v1.1 sequencing chemistry; a dilution buffer, BetterBuffer; and BigDye® XTerminator™. For software improvements, a barcoding system, auto fill worksheets; the LIMS (laboratory information management system); and expert system tools for mtDNA data management were designed and/or evaluated. The utilization of different robotic

NIJ Cooperative Agreement 2008-DNA-BX-K192

workstations has also been evaluated for mtDNA amplification, PCR product clean-up, and cycle sequencing reactions.

The objective of this project was to develop an integrated workflow from laboratory processing to data management for mtDNA sequence data. Several bottlenecks were addressed in the processing and analysis of mtDNA as it is currently performed in the casework laboratory for family reference samples (FRS section). The development of a new laboratory process with efficient amplification, sequencing, and analysis of mtDNA greatly enhances throughput capabilities, decreases unit costs, and significantly impacts the amount of time for laboratory processing and data review by the analyst. In addition, enhancements in the LIMS capabilities of auto fill worksheets and reagent calculations increase throughput and decrease human error.

Table of Contents

Executive Summary

Mitochondrial DNA analysis has proven to be an invaluable tool for victim identification from mass disasters and missing persons programs to criminal casework (Isenberg, 2004). The University of North Texas Health Science Center (UNTHSC) is primarily funded by the National Institute of Justice (NIJ) for the Missing Persons Program and uses advanced DNA technologies to process unidentified human remains and the family reference samples from biological relatives for both nuclear DNA (nDNA) and mtDNA. Since most missing persons cases rely heavily on mtDNA testing of skeletal remains, mtDNA testing of reference samples is necessary for making family associations. The resulting DNA profiles are uploaded to the Missing Persons Index database. In this database, mtDNA and nDNA profiles from the unidentified remains can be searched against the biological family reference profiles and associations are recommended through kinship analysis testing. There are several hundred thousand missing persons cases reported each year and there are more than 14,000 unidentified human skeletal remains retained in medical examiners' and coroners' offices nationwide (Rhonda K. Roby et al., 2007). These numbers alone demonstrate the throughput requirements needed for DNA processing.

Mitochondrial DNA testing is a laborious process which includes amplifying and sequencing two regions in the mtDNA genome (mtGenome) (Holland et al., 1995). The UNTHSC Field Testing Division (FTD) redesigned several steps for mtDNA amplification, sequencing, and purification procedures to increase efficiency, throughput capabilities, and reduce costs. Each step, or procedure, added, modified, or further optimized for high throughput processing has been validated. The current methods of mtDNA sample processing by the Family Reference Samples (FRS) section and the procedures proposed by FTD are displayed in Figure 1. As can be referenced in this diagram, robotic steps replace some of the manual processing performed by the FRS section. In addition, since a single amplicon is proposed in this workflow, fewer plates are generated and subjected to post-amplification purification. Fewer plates are also used in post-cycle sequencing purification. Sample processing methods are continually improving with advances in chemistry, instrumentation, and liquid handling robotics. Consequently, the rate of data generation exceeds that of data analysis, review, and reporting; hence, creating a bottleneck in the final review of data, reporting, and upload. Therefore, an expert system for high throughput data management has been developed.

Family Reference Sample Processing

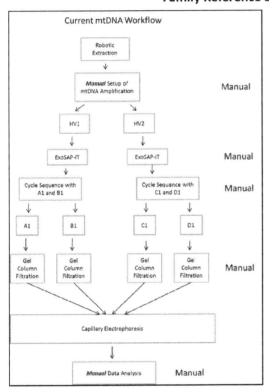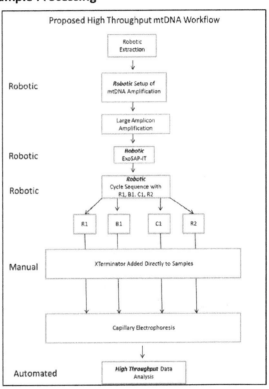

Figure 1. Comparison of the current mtDNA workflow used by the FRS section (flowchart on the left) to the proposed high throughput mtDNA workflow used by FTD (flowchart on the right). These changes include the use of additional robotic instrumentation, amplification of a single amplicon which amplifies the entire control region, XTerminator purification, and high throughput data analysis.

NIJ Cooperative Agreement 2008-DNA-BX-K192

Chemistry

FTD evaluated quantitative polymerase chain reaction (qPCR) assays for mtDNA quantification and redesigned several steps for mtDNA amplification, cycle sequencing, and purification procedures to increase efficiency, throughput capabilities, and reduce costs. Each step, or procedure, added, modified, or further optimized was included in this project, validated, and evaluated for increased efficiency.

mtDNA qPCR Assay

Introduction

The amount of mtDNA used for amplification and the quantity of amplified product for cycle sequencing is critical for obtaining high quality data. Too much product added to the cycle sequencing reaction results in noisy data and too little product generates low sequence signal. With an optimal amount of product added to the cycle sequencing assay, clean data are obtained with very little baseline noise. This is critical for efficient interpretation of data and high throughput sequence analysis. Additionally, if an optimal amount of DNA is added to the amplification reaction, downstream cycle sequencing procedures can be standardized. This will also limit the amount of sample DNA extract consumed. Conservation of valuable sample extract is paramount when analyzing forensic samples. Thus, the need for a quantification assay for human mtDNA is evident.

A human mtDNA qPCR assay (Kavlick *et al.*, In Press) with two simultaneous amplifications was validated. The first amplification targets a 105 base pair sequence located in the coding region. The second amplification is an exogenous internal positive control. The method used for this assay is based on absolute quantification and utilizes a DNA standard dilution series of known quantities to generate a standard curve from which the quantities of mtDNA in samples may be determined.

Materials and Methods

For the internal validation studies, DNA extracts from 43 non-probative bone DNA extracts were tested. In addition, DNA from a single donor was extracted using an organic protocol and purified with ethanol precipitation. Controls were run in duplicate with each assay; these controls included positive controls of human genomic DNA from cell line HL60 (ATCC, Manassas, VA), reagent controls, and no template controls.

This qPCR assay utilizes TaqMan® MGB Probe (Applied Biosystems, Foster City, CA) chemistry. The mtDNA target for this assay is a 105 base pair region within the NADH dehydrogenase subunit 5 (MT-ND5) gene which corresponds to positions 13,288 to 13,392 of the revised Cambridge Reference Sequence (rCRS) (Andrews *et al.*, 1999). For the standard curve, a 115 base ultramer DNA oligonucleotide (Integrated DNA Technologies, Coralville, IA), of known concentration, was used to generate eight standards covering a range of 0.0001pg/μL (6 mtDNA copies/μL) to 1,000pg/μL (58,830,674 mtDNA copies/μL) of mtDNA. A TaqMan® Exogenous Internal Positive Control (Applied Biosystems) is included in this assay and is used to detect inhibition. Amplification and detection were performed on a 7500 Real-Time PCR System (Applied Biosystems) and Sequence Detection System (SDS) Software v1.2.3 (Applied Biosystems) following the manufacturer's default thermal cycling protocol.

Extracted DNA from 43 non-probative bone samples and their corresponding reagent blanks were quantified and compared to the relative number of bases reported (Figure 2). For precision and reproducibility, this assay was repeated 15 times for the standards and controls which were run in duplicate (Table 1 and Figure 3). Based on these studies, standard curve parameters were established for acceptable slope, R^2, and Y-intercept values. Performance of the lowest standard was evaluated to determine the sensitivity of this assay (Table 1). Inhibition studies were conducted to evaluate the performance of this assay in the presence of three known PCR inhibitors often encountered with forensic casework samples: humic acid, hematin, and melanin. Nine concentrations for each inhibitor [humic acid (0 to 30 ng/µL); hematin (0 to 30 µM); and melanin (0 to 30 ng/µL)] were tested with varying concentrations of mtDNA (Table 2).

Results

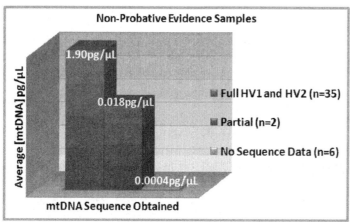

Figure 2. Of the 43 bone DNA extracts assayed, 35 produced a full mtDNA sequence profile (HV1 and HV2) with an average mtDNA quantification value of 1.90pg/µL. Two samples yielded only partial sequence data (of low quality) and had an average mtDNA quantification value of 0.018pg/µL. Finally, six samples, with an average mtDNA quantification value of 0.0004pg/µL, failed to produce any sequence data.

	Precision and Sensitivity pg/µL							
	1,000	100	10	1.0	0.1	0.01	0.001	0.0001
	STD 1	STD 2	STD 3	STD 4	STD 5	STD 6	STD 7	STD 8
Mean Ct	12.09	15.86	19.39	22.85	26.34	29.60	32.76	35.25
SD	0.27	0.27	0.25	0.27	0.30	0.35	0.46	0.96
Minimum	11.48	15.29	19.06	22.33	25.8	29.06	32.17	33.67
Maximum	12.92	16.29	20.11	23.5	27.04	30.42	34.1	36.92

Table 1. Cycle threshold (Ct) values and their standard deviations (SD) exhibit an inverse relationship with mtDNA concentration. Standard 8, the lowest concentrated standard (0.0001pg/µL), exhibited the widest range and highest SD of Ct values. The lowest standard was always detected and resulted in an average Ct value of 35.25. This Ct value is well within the 40 cycles performed with this assay, giving a sensitivity of detection of 0.0001pg/µL.

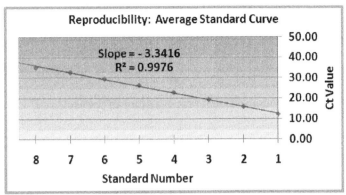

Figure 3. Reproducibility was measured by evaluating the results in duplicate of the standard curve for
15 repeated runs. The standard curve was created by averaging the Ct values (n=30) for each of
Standard 1 through Standard 8. Linear regression analysis was performed to calculate the slope and R^2
value. Amplification efficiency was 99.18%.

Assay Tolerance of Known PCR Inhibitors			
	Humic Acid 0.5 ng/µL	Hematin 1µM	Melanin 0.05 ng/µL
20.0	☑	☑	☑
2.0	☑	☑	☑
0.002	☒	☒	☑
0.0002	☒	☒	☒

Table 2. Inhibition was determined by comparing the Ct values of non-treated samples to the Ct values
of the treated samples. An increase of the average Ct value + 1SD was indicative of partial inhibition (☑)
and no detection of Ct value was indicative of complete inhibition (☒). This assay's tolerance threshold
for humic acid, hematin, and melanin are 0.5ng/µL, 1µM, and 0.05ng/µL, respectively. At these
concentrations of inhibitor, partial inhibition or complete inhibition is expected depending on the
amount of template mtDNA.

Conclusion

This assay successfully demonstrated its utility for quantifying mtDNA for forensic casework

samples. It also exhibited a high degree of precision and reproducibility evidenced by consistent cycle

threshold (Ct) values of the standards and controls for all 15 repeated runs. The lowest standard was

always detected with an average cycle threshold value of 35.25; this is well within the 40 cycles performed with this assay giving it a sensitivity of 0.0001pg/μL. In the presence of various concentrations of three different inhibitors, this assay successfully produced results at various levels of template mtDNA. The successful completion of this validation study demonstrates the suitability of the human mtDNA qPCR assay for use in forensic casework and identification of human remains.

mtDNA Amplification and Cycle Sequencing

Introduction

Mitochondrial DNA processing includes amplifying and sequencing two regions of the mtGenome. In forensic analysis, two hypervariable regions are analyzed; these are referred to as HV1 and HV2. Currently, the FRS section uses the following methods for processing family reference samples:

- After extraction, both HV1 and HV2 regions are amplified in two separate 25μL reactions, requiring 10μL of DNA extract for each reaction.

- Amplified products are purified with 5μL of ExoSAP-IT® (USB Corp., Cleveland, OH) and cycle sequenced using a full-volume reaction with the ABI PRISM® dRhodamine Terminator Cycle Sequencing Kit.

- Following cycle sequencing, samples are purified using Performa® DTR (dye terminator removal) Ultra 96-well plates (Edge BioSystems, Gaithersburg, MD) and electrophoresed on the ABI PRISM® 3130*xl* Genetic Analyzer.

This method uses an excessive amount of DNA extract, requires several sample transfers, and is costly; in addition, the sequencing chemistry availability is threatened by discontinuance by the manufacturer.

Materials and Methods

In order to decrease the number of sample transfers as well as the amount of DNA extract required for mtDNA amplification, new amplification primers were evaluated. Primers R1 and R2 encompass both the HV1 and HV2 regions (Figure 4).

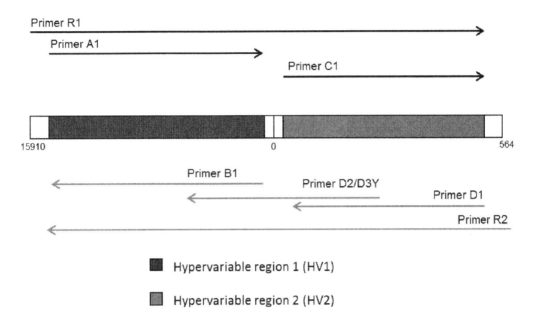

Figure 4. Control region of mtDNA and primers used by the FRS section and/or FTD. The FRS section uses primers A1 and B1 to amplify the HV1 region and primers C1 and D1 to amplify the HV2 region. FTD uses primers R1 and R2 to amplify the large amplicon, encompassing the HV1 and HV2 regions, and generating additional base information. The D2 and D3Y primers are discussed in the next section.

Since one of the costly reagents is ExoSAP-IT®, a decrease in the amount of ExoSAP-IT® required to appropriately purify the product was evaluated. ExoSAP-IT® is used to remove excess primer and excess dNTPs (Bell, 2008). The modifications to this procedure involved decreasing the total concentration of amplification primers from 6µM to 2.7µM per reaction. The amount of dNTPs was also decreased from 8mM to 6mM. Additionally, to obtain optimal amounts of amplified mtDNA with no excess product, the amplification cycle number was evaluated and decreased from 32 cycles to 28 cycles. These changes allow for the decrease in the amount of ExoSAP-IT® required to appropriately purify the PCR product. The validated procedure decreases ExoSAP-IT® from a total of 10µL to 2µL per sample.

Additional cost savings were noted in the cycle sequencing step. The dRhodamine kit is an expensive kit and the manufacturer has announced its intent to discontinue this product. A reduced reaction volume using the BigDye® Terminator v1.1 Cycle Sequencing Kit (Applied Biosystems) was evaluated. BigDye® v1.1 was chosen since it sequences closer to the primer (Applied Biosystems, 2002). Also, post-cycle sequencing purification using the BigDye® XTerminator™ Purification Kit (Applied Biosystems) was validated using a reduced reaction volume (Applied Biosystems, 2006).

Extracted DNA using the DNA IQ™ System (Promega Corp., Madison, WI) does not provide the range of optimal DNA. Therefore, the Quantifiler™ Human DNA Quantification Kit (Applied Biosystems) for total nDNA was introduced into the process since the mtDNA qPCR assay had not yet been designed or validated. In order to reduce costs, a reduced reaction volume of this kit was validated. Quantification was then followed by normalization of the extract to achieve more consistent results among samples.

Conclusion

In conclusion, several steps for mtDNA amplification, cycle sequencing, and purification procedures were redesigned in order to increase throughput capabilities and reduce costs. After normalizing the samples, amplification of the large amplicon is performed. Post-amplification cleanup is carried out using a reduced amount of ExoSAP-IT® added directly to the amplified product. The purified products are then prepared for fluorescence-based cycle sequencing with a reduced reaction volume using the BigDye® Terminator v1.1 Cycle Sequencing Kit. To further enhance the quality of sequence data obtained by reducing the sequencing chemistry, an enhancer buffer, BetterBuffer (Gel Company Inc., San Francisco, CA), is used in the cycle sequencing reaction. After cycle sequencing, samples are purified using the BigDye® XTerminator™ Purification Kit. The purification master mix is added directly to the cycle sequenced product. After samples and purification master mix are thoroughly combined, the samples are ready for capillary electrophoresis on the 3130xl with no need of time-consuming sample transfer such as those conducted with the Performa® DTR Ultra 96-well plates. The quality of data obtained from the procedure validated by FTD, and the quality of data obtained using the original method is shown in Figure 5. There is a reduction in the number of transfers performed in implementing this procedure by four transfers and a significant reduction in the consumables and reagents used.

dRhodamine: Full Volume Reaction

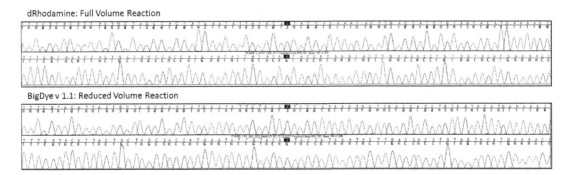

BigDye v 1.1: Reduced Volume Reaction

Figure 5. Sequence data obtained using dRhodamine in the FRS section compared to sequence data obtained using the BigDye® v1.1 method validated by FTD.

The quality of the data generated by this procedure is occasionally of a lesser quality than the data generated by the dRhodamine procedure used by the FRS section. Two of the most commonly observed artifacts are excessive dyes which are not removed (Figure 6) and noisy sequence data obtained when too much input DNA is amplified (Figure 7).

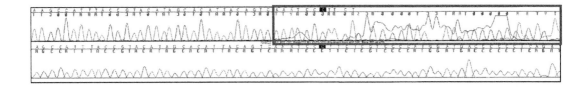

Figure 6. Sequence data obtained using the FTD method. The excess unremoved dyes are highlighted in the red box and are caused by poor mixing of the post-cycle sequencing purification chemistry. This artifact is not observed using the FRS section procedure with Performa® DTR Ultra 96-well plates.

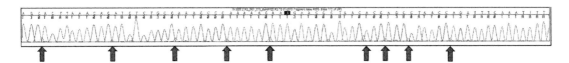

Figure 7. Sequence data obtained using the FTD method when too much DNA is amplified. Extra peaks are denoted by the red arrows. This is not seen with the FRS section procedures using dRhodamine.

A study was performed by FTD on the Tecan Freedom EVO® 200, comparing the sequence data obtained from FRS to the data obtained from the validated procedures used by FTD. These data are presented in the "Overall Validation Study: Tecan Freedom EVO® 200" section. Despite the differences observed in the sequence quality, this procedure is recommended. More studies should be conducted to address these artifacts.

Additional Primer Design Study

Polymorphisms commonly occur at the D2 primer binding site (see Figure 4), namely 295 C to T and a two base pair deletion at positions 290 and 291. These base changes decrease amplification and cycle sequencing efficiency when using the D2 primer. Consequently, retesting is required which hinders high throughput efforts. There are instances where a portion of HV2 was not reported for casework samples due to these primer binding site mutations. Primer D2 was redesigned; this redesign was necessary to maximize amplification efficiency and minimize loss of sequence information for this highly polymorphic region. A degenerate primer, D3Y, was designed, ordered, and validated. This primer was designed for amplification and sequencing of all samples types, *i.e.,* family reference samples and/or evidence.

Testing was performed to demonstrate amplification recovery using a variety of polymorphic samples (Figure 8). Additionally, the primer was tested on two casework samples, a paraffin embedded tissue and a bone. The casework analyst was not able to report a portion of HV2 due to amplification failure; however, using D3Y, complete sequence data were obtained for this region (Figure 9).

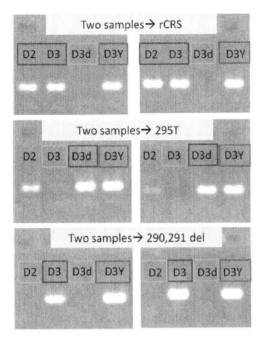

Figure 8. Amplification recovery using D3Y. D2 is the primer currently used for HV2 in the FRS and casework sections. The redesigned primer D3Y contains two primers: D3 which binds perfectly for samples with 295C (the published base in the rCRS) and D3d, the degenerate version of D3, which binds perfectly to samples with 295T. Both D3 and D3d accommodate samples with and without the 290, 291 deletion. The blue boxes indicate which single primer is the perfect match for amplification of the samples. The yellow boxes indicate amplification failure. The D3Y lanes are highlighted with green boxes, the only primer where amplification success is seen for all sample types.

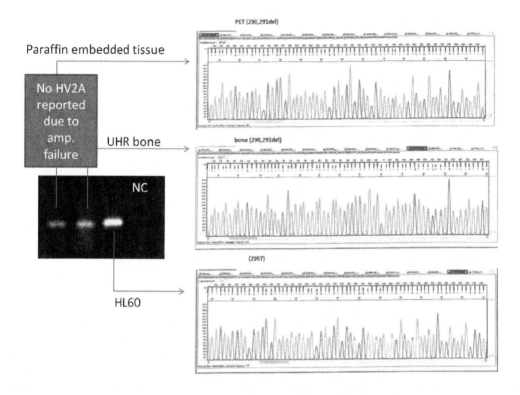

Figure 9. Amplification and sequence recovery using primer D3Y.

Software

To further streamline automation and reduce entry errors, barcoding, automated sample tracking, and auto-population of sample sheets has been a key focus in the FTD laboratory for increased efficiency. These automated sheets include extraction, quantification, normalization, and 3130*xl* upload worksheets to reduce time and error in sample entry (Phillips *et al.*, 2009; R. K. Roby *et al.*, 2009). The use of filter metrics to quickly assess mtDNA sequence data has also been introduced. These filter metrics have been incorporated for data screening using expert system rule firing features (Curtis *et al.*, 2010). Lastly, the calculations performed for casework in the LIMS software has been validated.

Barcoding

Barcoding software was developed to allow the user to electronically track samples in real-time. The system provides a highly detailed electronic trail for all samples. Upon receiving a sample, the submitting barcode is scanned, or sample entry is performed manually, and a unique barcode is assigned (Figure 10). This barcode is then placed on the sample package or container. All original information and future information associated with this sample are stored in an electronic database. For family reference samples, when enough samples are received to create a batch, the system alerts the analyst. As the analyst scans the samples to be processed, the software creates the batch layout. This layout is saved and all processes performed on this batch maintain the same layout. In order to appropriately track the batch through the processes, the software generates new plate barcodes for each process, performed; this barcode allows for more simplistic sample tracking and a reduction in transcription errors.

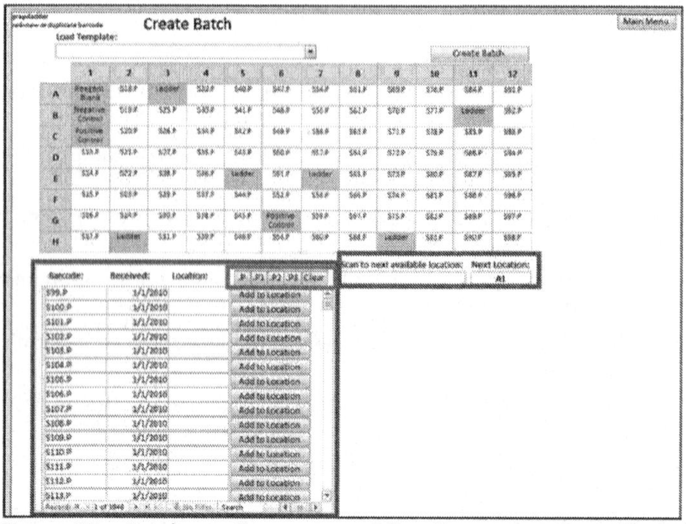

Figure 10. Batch creation menu. After the analyst is notified that enough samples are present to
process a batch, a sample list is generated (red box). The analyst can also filter the samples based on
sample type (green box). There are two approaches to creating a batch. The analyst can choose the
appropriate plate template and select "add to location" and the samples will auto fill into the next
available location of the 96-well plate or the analyst can scan the samples (blue box) and the samples
will auto fill into the next available well.

To further simplify laboratory processing, the software automatically calculates the volume of

reagents needed for each step. In addition to barcoding samples, instruments and reagents are also

barcoded. During each process the necessary reagents and required instruments are scanned; the

appropriate information is retrieved from the information database and imported to the worksheet.

These barcoding steps decrease the chance for human error (*e.g.*, transcription errors), are faster to

enter, and are easier to read than handwriting. This system performs important quality control

measures of reagents (*e.g.*, notification of reagent in-service and whether or not the reagent is expired).

Automated Worksheets

Automated sample tracking and worksheets were developed using Microsoft Office® Excel.

Sample names are manually entered into the *Samples* tab of the spreadsheet and do not need to be entered again, reducing the possibility of human error downstream (Figure 11). Subsequent processing worksheets for extraction, quantification, normalization, amplification, cycle sequencing, and analysis are auto-populated in order to streamline sample processing.

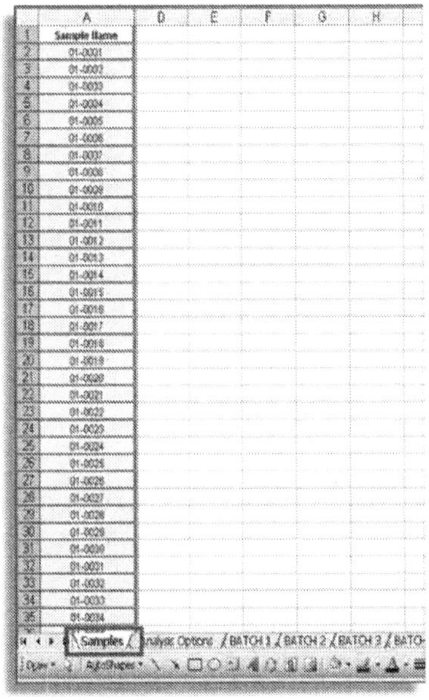

Figure 11. The *Samples* tab displayed is the one and only time a sample name requires manual entry.

The *Extraction/Cutting Plate* layout guides the analyst in swab cutting placement and the master mix calculations are performed automatically for use with DNA IQ™ System on the Tecan Freedom EVO® 100 (Figure 12). Quantification and normalization are performed after extraction. A *7500 upload* spreadsheet (saved as a .txt file) was developed for import of samples into the SDS v1.2.3, further improving efficiency (Figure 13). Quantification results can be imported into the *Quant outputs* tab of the normalization spreadsheet. The plate layout is auto-populated and displays the sample name and three values: 1) the quantification result; 2) the volume of extracted DNA needed in microliters; and, 3) the volume of diluent needed in microliters to achieve the desired volume and optimal concentration for downstream processes (Figure 14).

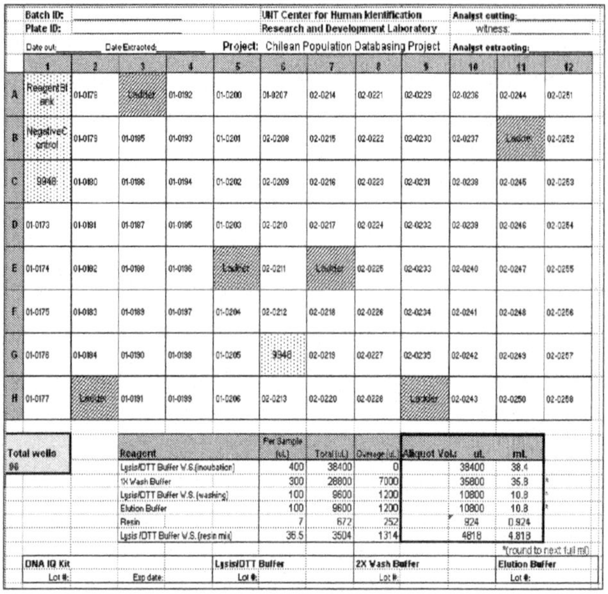

Batch ID: ____ UNT Center for Human Identification Analyst cutting: ____
Plate ID: ____ Research and Development Laboratory witness: ____
Date out: ____ Date Extracted: ____ Project: Chilean Population Databasing Project Analyst extracting: ____

	1	2	3	4	5	6	7	8	9	10	11	12
A	ReagentBl ank	01-0178	Ladder	01-0192	01-0200	01-0207	02-0214	02-0221	02-0229	02-0236	02-0244	02-0251
B	NegativeC ontrol	01-0179	01-0185	01-0193	01-0201	02-0208	02-0215	02-0222	02-0230	02-0237	Ladder	02-0252
C	9948	01-0180	01-0186	01-0194	01-0202	02-0209	02-0216	02-0223	02-0231	02-0238	02-0245	02-0253
D	01-0173	01-0181	01-0187	01-0195	01-0203	02-0210	02-0217	02-0224	02-0232	02-0239	02-0246	02-0254
E	01-0174	01-0182	01-0188	01-0196	Ladder	02-0211	Ladder	02-0225	02-0233	02-0240	02-0247	02-0255
F	01-0175	01-0183	01-0189	01-0197	01-0204	02-0212	02-0218	02-0226	02-0234	02-0241	02-0248	02-0256
G	01-0176	01-0184	01-0190	01-0198	01-0205	9948	02-0219	02-0227	02-0235	02-0242	02-0249	02-0257
H	01-0177	Ladder	01-0191	01-0199	01-0206	02-0213	02-0220	02-0228	Ladder	02-0243	02-0250	02-0258

Total wells 96

Reagent	Per Sample (uL)	Total (uL)	Overage (uL)	Aliquot Vol.: uL	mL	
Lysis/DTT Buffer V.S.(incubation)	400	38400	0	38400	38.4	
1X Wash Buffer	300	28800	7000	35800	35.8	*
Lysis/DTT Buffer V.S. (washing)	100	9600	1200	10800	10.8	*
Elution Buffer	100	9600	1200	10800	10.8	*
Resin	7	672	252	924	0.924	
Lysis /DTT Buffer V.S. (resin mix)	36.5	3504	1314	4818	4.818	

*(round to next full ml)

DNA IQ Kit		Lysis/DTT Buffer	2X Wash Buffer	Elution Buffer
Lot #:	Exp date:	Lot #:	Lot #:	Lot #:

Figure 12. The *Extraction/Cutting Plate* layout aids the analyst in placement of the appropriate sample when cutting the sample swab; the layout also automatically performs master mix component calculations.

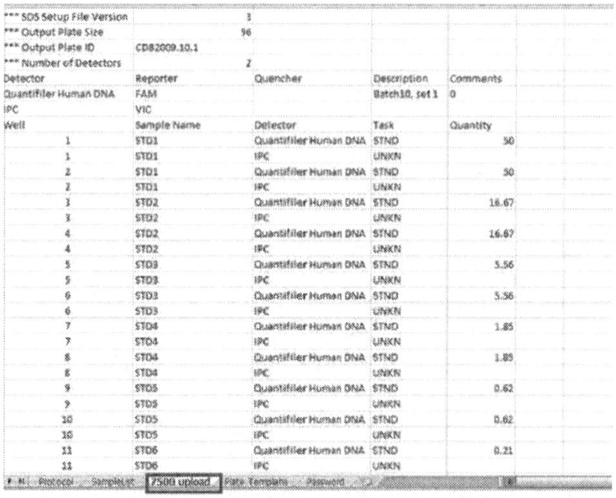

*** SDS Setup File Version	3			
*** Output Plate Size	96			
*** Output Plate ID	CD82009.10.1			
*** Number of Detectors	2			
Detector	Reporter	Quencher	Description	Comments
Quantifiler Human DNA	FAM		Batch10, set 1	0
IPC	VIC			
Well	Sample Name	Detector	Task	Quantity
1	STD1	Quantifiler Human DNA	STND	50
1	STD1	IPC	UNKN	
2	STD1	Quantifiler Human DNA	STND	50
2	STD1	IPC	UNKN	
3	STD2	Quantifiler Human DNA	STND	16.67
3	STD2	IPC	UNKN	
4	STD2	Quantifiler Human DNA	STND	16.67
4	STD2	IPC	UNKN	
5	STD3	Quantifiler Human DNA	STND	5.56
5	STD3	IPC	UNKN	
6	STD3	Quantifiler Human DNA	STND	5.56
6	STD3	IPC	UNKN	
7	STD4	Quantifiler Human DNA	STND	1.85
7	STD4	IPC	UNKN	
8	STD4	Quantifiler Human DNA	STND	1.85
8	STD4	IPC	UNKN	
9	STD5	Quantifiler Human DNA	STND	0.62
9	STD5	IPC	UNKN	
10	STD5	Quantifiler Human DNA	STND	0.62
10	STD5	IPC	UNKN	
11	STD6	Quantifiler Human DNA	STND	0.21
11	STD6	IPC	UNKN	

Figure 13. Copying and pasting the sample names from the initial *Samples* tab into the *SampleList* tab of the 7500 upload spreadsheet reduces human error when manually entering sample names into the SDS plate layout. The user can save the *7500 upload* tab as a .txt file and import all necessary information into the SDS software.

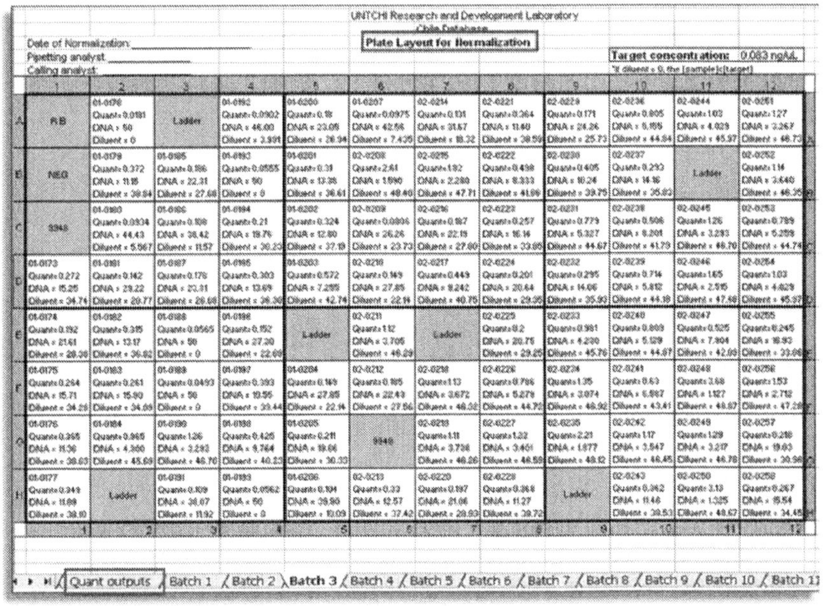

Figure 14. The quantification results are exported as a .csv file from the SDS software can be imported into the *Quant outputs* tab of the plate layout for normalization. The *Batch #* tab displays the plate layout and all necessary volumes for performing sample normalization.

The plate layout for all steps remains the same throughout the entire process, except quantification due to wells needed on the plate for quantification standards. Master mix calculations are performed automatically in worksheets for amplification and cycle sequencing (Figures 15 and 16). Capillary electrophoresis is performed on the ABI PRISM® 3130*xl* Genetic Analyzer. Under the *Analysis Options* tab in the spreadsheet, the analysis type (*i.e.,* Identifiler, Yfiler, or Sequencing) can be selected which modifies the sample name with the appropriate analysis extension (*e.g.,* "SAMPLE.**ID**" for Identifiler) and the template is automatically formatted for upload to the 3130*xl* Data Collection Software. The final spreadsheet located under the appropriate *Batch #* tab is auto-populated from the initial *Samples* tab and represents the plate layout for capillary electrophoresis.

UNT Center for Human Identification
Procedure Manual – Research & Development Laboratory

Amplification Setup for Identifiler, Yfiler and mtDNA on the MiniPrep 75

Batch ID: CDB2009-05 Project: CHILEAN POPULATION DATABASE
Sample #: 90

Identifiler Master Mix	Kit Lot #		Exp Date		
Reagent	Sample #	Calculations			Total
Identifiler PCR Reaction Mix	90	X 5.8µL =	522	X 1.30 =	679 µL
Identifiler Primer Set	90	X 2.9µL =	261	X 1.30 =	339 µL
Polymerase	90	X 0.3µL =	27	X 1.30 =	35.1 µL

Yfiler Master Mix	Kit Lot #		Exp Date		
Reagent	Sample #	Calculations			Total
Yfiler PCR Reaction Mix	90	X 5.8µL =	522	X 1.30 =	679 µL
Yfiler Primer Set	90	X 2.9µL =	261	X 1.30 =	339 µL
Polymerase	90	X 0.3µL =	27	X 1.30 =	35.1 µL

mtDNA Master Mix							
Reagent	Lot #	Exp. Date	Sample #	Calculations			Total
ddH2O			90	X 2.7µL =	243	X 1.35 =	328.1 µL
10X GeneAmp PCR Buffer II			90	X 1.5µL =	135	X 1.35 =	182.3 µL
1.6 mg/mL BSA			90	X 1.5µL =	135	X 1.35 =	182.3 µL
10mM dNTPs			90	X 1.2µL =	108	X 1.35 =	145.8 µL
25mM MgCl2			90	X 0.9µL =	81	X 1.35 =	109.4 µL
Polymerase			90	X 0.6µL =	54	X 1.35 =	72.9 µL
10uM R1 Primer			90	X 0.3µL =	27	X 1.35 =	36.45 µL
10uM R2 Primer			90	X 0.3µL =	27	X 1.35 =	36.45 µL

Figure 15. Master mix components for Identifiler, Yfiler, and mtDNA amplification are automatically calculated saving the analyst time and improving laboratory efficiency.

UNT Center for Human Identification
Procedure Manual – Research & Development Laboratory

High Throughput Cycle Sequencing Worksheet

Batch ID: CDB2009-003 Project: Chilean Population Database
Sample #: 100

Post-Amp Clean-Up	Date:		Analyst		Thermal Cycler #
Reagent	Lot #	Exp. Date	Sample #		Total
ExoSAP-IT			100	X 2µL=	200 µL

Cycle Sequencing					
Reagent	Lot #	Exp. Date	Sample #		Total
BigDye Terminator v1.1			100	X 1µL=	100 µL
[illegible] Buffer			100	X 5µL=	500 µL
Primer			100	X 1.5µL=	150 µL
ddH2O			100	X 6.5µL=	650 µL

XTerminator Purification					
Reagent	Lot #	Exp. Date	Sample #		Total
XTerminator			100	X 3.7µL=	370 µL
SAM Solution			100	X 16.4µL=	1640 µL
ddH2O			100	X 35µL=	3500 µL

Primer	R1	F1	C1	R2	A4	B4	C2	D2
Lot #								
Exp. Date								

Figure 16. Post-amplification processes and the necessary master mix calculations are calculated for the analyst on the Cycle Sequencing Worksheet.

LIMS Validation

LISA (Laboratory Information Systems Applications) is a LIMS designed by Future Technologies Incorporated (FTI) (Fairfax, VA) for the management and analysis of genetic data from forensic casework, mass fatality incident investigations, research, and other special investigations. LISA is composed of several modules: Case Management; Lab Processing; Systems Administration; and Statistical Analysis.

Validation studies and other tests were conducted to verify the algorithms and calculations performed in the Statistical Analysis module. The Core Stats, Kinship Analysis, Mito Analysis, Mixture Statistics, and Searching algorithms were subjected to rigorous testing, bug reporting, and then re-testing and re-evaluation. The Core Stats feature performs statistical calculations typically associated with forensic casework. For example, Core Stats calculates the random match probability and frequency of a DNA profile. It calculates the likelihood ratio (LR) for a potential familial relationship (*e.g.*, parent-child, sibling, or other) tested between two or more profiles using all genetic data available. The Core Stats feature (Figure 17) generates reports of DNA profiles and results and the equations used to make the calculations.

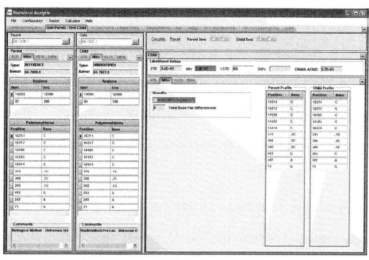

Figure 17. Core Stats feature performs routine forensic calculations.

The Kinship Analysis feature (Figure 18) has tools that can assist an analyst in designing a missing person's family pedigree(s) in an efficient manner using an integrated third party program Progeny© Software (Progeny Software Inc., Wolfville, Nova Scotia). The analyst can first build the pedigree, label the individuals in the pedigree, and then add the DNA profiles to the pedigree. An analyst can use the Kinship Analysis module to edit, build, and save multiple pedigrees in one file for a case set to be assembled into an investigation file.

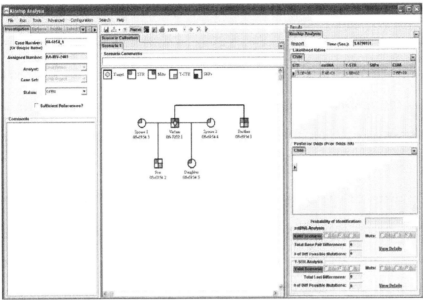

Figure 18. Kinship Analysis feature assists the analyst in designing the family pedigrees.

After building a pedigree, the analyst can then analyze the pedigree to obtain a cumulative LR. After the analysis, LISA provides the analyst with a breakdown of the LR results for each type of genetic system and population group tested. These calculations were performed for many pedigrees and compared to PopStats 5.4, Kin CALc 3.1, and the MPKin programs for the validation studies.

eFAST™ Software

Introduction

Sequence analysis is a time-consuming process, particularly due to the large amount of data that are required to obtain a complete profile. The standards for mtDNA sequencing for forensic casework require double coverage for all bases reported in an mtDNA profile. For one sample, a minimum of four traces must be generated, evaluated for quality, and, if the traces are of acceptable quality, assembled to the rCRS. The quality screening process used for casework is monotonous, subjective, and time-consuming. eFAST™ Software v1.1 was designed to replace the repetitive and subjective process of screening sequence data with an expert system approach based on optimized filter metrics (R. Roby, Phillips, Thomas, Keppler, & Eisenberg, 2010). eFAST™ Software provides: 1) customizable trace name pattern analysis (Figure 19); 2) objective quality assessment of controls and traces (Figure 20); 3) automated file distribution (Figure 21); 4) sample progress summaries to facilitate laboratory workflow (Figure 21); and, 5) electronic notification of run performance via email (Figure 22).

eFAST™ Software calculates a Contiguous Read Length (CRL) and Trace Score (TS) for each trace. CRL is calculated as the number of uninterrupted bases in the trace that have a quality value (QV) of greater than 20. TS is the average QV of the bases that remain in the trace (after trimming). These metrics are used to sort traces into three categories: high quality (HQ), review (REV), and low quality (LQ). These metrics are used to evaluate the trace quality of both controls and sample traces. The user can define the sample naming convention, set the thresholds in a primer-specific manner, and can define custom primers. Other customizable features make eFAST™ Software amenable for all dRhodamine and BigDye® sequencing applications.

During a plate run, eFAST™ Software evaluates controls as soon as the data collection is complete for each run. If a control fails early in the plate, an Early Warning email is generated and sent to alert the user of the problem. If the controls do not fail, eFAST™ Software creates a summary email for the user once data collection for a plate is complete. This email informs the user of the number of traces qualified as HQ, REV, and LQ. Additionally, the email summarizes the performance of the controls.

eFAST™ Software provides a color-coded interface which can be filtered to only display traces in need of review (REV). Once the analyst has assigned the quality of the REV traces manually, all of the sample trace files are automatically sorted into pre-defined directories. The traces categorized as LQ are archived in a directory titled *Low Quality*, and the HQ traces for each sample are grouped for analysis. After distribution, eFAST™ Software creates a Sample Report which indicates the status of all traces for each sample. The Sample Report can be sorted and exported; it is designed to facilitate subsequent laboratory processing to further increase efficiency.

An efficiency and performance evaluation study using eFAST™ Software v1.1 was performed. The purpose of this assessment was to: 1) quantify the potential time savings obtained using automated filter metrics and 2) assess the accuracy of the sorting algorithms employed by eFAST™ Software v1.1.

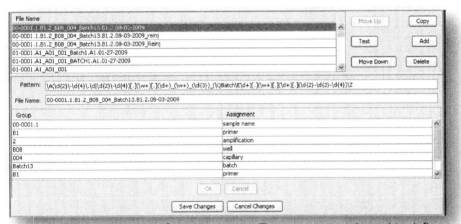

Figure 19. Pattern generator for trace names. The name pattern is used to define each handle of the trace name in order to automate sample grouping, control assessment, and primer-specific quality assessments.

Automatically parsed Sample Name and Primer

Trace File Name	Sample Name	Primer	TS	CRL	Status	
NegativeControl_B01_003_Batch122.R1.12-31-2010.ab1	NC	R1	0	0	HQ	Control evaluation: Negative Control (NC), Reagent Blank (RB), and Positive Control (PC)
ReagentBlank_A01_001_Batch122.R1.12-31-2010.ab1	RB	R1	0	0	HQ	
10-3557.2.R1_B03_003_Batch122.R1.12-31-2010.ab1	10-3557.2	R1	35	269	REV	
10-3560.1.R1_C03_005_Batch122.R1.12-31-2010.ab1	10-3560.1	R1	36	239	REV	
10-3566.1.R1_D03_007_Batch122.R1.12-31-2010.ab1	10-3566.1	R1	35	590	HQ	
10-3571.1.R1_E03_009_Batch122.R1.12-31-2010.ab1	10-3571.1	R1	0	0	LQ	
10-3572.1.R1_F03_011_Batch122.R1.12-31-2010.ab1	10-3572.1	R1	35	611	HQ	Ex: trace that passes automatically based on filter metrics; no analyst review needed.
10-3575.1.R1_G03_013_Batch122.R1.12-31-2010.ab1	10-3575.1	R1	35	568	HQ	
10-3576.1.R1_H03_015_Batch122.R1.12-31-2010.ab1	10-3576.1	R1	31	577	HQ	
10-3577.1.R1_A04_002_Batch122.R1.12-31-2010.ab1	10-3577.1	R1	34	532	HQ	
10-3578.1.R1_B04_004_Batch122.R1.12-31-2010.ab1	10-3578.1	R1	35	559	HQ	
10-3588.1.R1_C04_006_Batch122.R1.12-31-2010.ab1	10-3588.1	R1	35	584	HQ	
10-3594.1.R1_D04_008_Batch122.R1.12-31-2010.ab1	10-3594.1	R1	35	553	HQ	
10-3596.1.R1_E04_010_Batch122.R1.12-31-2010.ab1	10-3596.1	R1	36	261	REV	
10-3598.1.R1_F04_012_Batch122.R1.12-31-2010.ab1	10-3598.1	R1	33	566	HQ	Ex: trace that falls in the REVIEW threshold; analyst review is needed
10-3603.1.R1_G04_014_Batch122.R1.12-31-2010.ab1	10-3603.1	R1	35	520	HQ	
10-3604.1.R1_H04_016_Batch122.R1.12-31-2010.ab1	10-3604.1	R1	29	486	LQ	
06-4047.2.R1_A06_002_Batch122.R1.12-31-2010.ab1	06-4047.2	R1	31	524	HQ	
08-6307.2.R1_B06_004_Batch122.R1.12-31-2010.ab1	08-6307.2	R1	36	497	HQ	Ex: trace that automatically fails based on filter metrics; no analyst review needed.
10-2394.2.R1_C06_006_Batch122.R1.12-31-2010.ab1	10-2394.2	R1	35	578	HQ	
10-2911.2.R1_D06_008_Batch122.R1.12-31-2010.ab1	10-2911.2	R1	33	225	REV	
10-2911.3.R1_E06_010_Batch122.R1.12-31-2010.ab1	10-2911.3	R1	33	222	REV	
10-3022.2.R1_F06_012_Batch122.R1.12-31-2010.ab1	10-3022.2	R1	35	525	HQ	
10-3056.2.R1_H06_016_Batch122.R1.12-31-2010.ab1	10-3056.2	R1	34	579	HQ	
10-3606.1.R1_A05_001_Batch122.R1.12-31-2010.ab1	10-3606.1	R1	35	564	HQ	
10-3609.3.R1_B05_003_Batch122.R1.12-31-2010.ab1	10-3609.3	R1	35	271	REV	
10-3610.1.R1_C05_005_Batch122.R1.12-31-2010.ab1	10-3610.1	R1	35	607	HQ	
10-3611.1.R1_D05_007_Batch122.R1.12-31-2010.ab1	10-3611.1	R1	35	574	HQ	
10-3647.2.R1_F05_011_Batch122.R1.12-31-2010.ab1	10-3647.2	R1	35	526	HQ	
10-3885.1.R1_G05_013_Batch122.R1.12-31-2010.ab1	10-3885.1	R1	35	594	HQ	
10-3923.1.R1_H05_015_Batch122.R1.12-31-2010.ab1	10-3923.1	R1	35	526	HQ	
HL60_G06_014_Batch122.R1.12-31-2010.ab1	PC	R1	29	528	LQ	

Figure 20. Automated and objective quality assessment of controls and traces.

NIJ Cooperative Agreement 2008-DNA-BX-K192

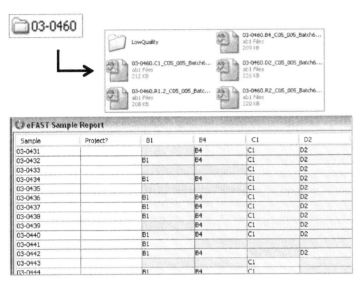

Figure 21.   Automated file distribution and Sample Report. eFAST™ Software automatically creates a directory for every sample processed, based on the defined trace naming pattern. Within this directory, traces classified as HQ are grouped and traces that were classified as LQ are archived in a sub-directory. The sample directories are summarized in the Sample Report to facilitate subsequent sample processing. The red cells indicate that the sample does not have a high quality trace for this primer, while the green cell indicates that the primer sequenced successfully.

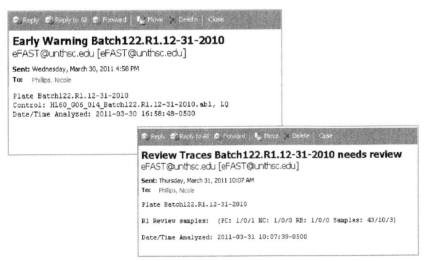

Figure 22. eFAST™ Software sends automated email notifications which include early warnings for a control failure as well as plate completion summaries. These plate completion summaries provide an overview of the run's performance.

Efficiency and Performance Evaluation

Methods

Data used for this study were generated in the FTD using standard operating procedures for high

throughput sample processing. Two methods were used to evaluate 344 sequence traces (172

generated using the R1 primer and 172 generated using the A4 primer), and compared for efficiency and

accuracy.

Method 1 is representative of the procedure used by the FRS section. For sequence quality

assessment under this method, the analyst launches all traces in Sequencher™ v4.8 (Gene Codes

Corporation, Ann Arbor, MI) and views each trace in the chromatogram viewer window. The analyst

notes which traces are of acceptable quality (passing) and which traces needed further action (failing).

All 344 traces were viewed and assessed in this manner for this study and the entire process was timed.

Method 2 uses eFAST™ Software to automate the screening process. For sequence quality

assessment under this method, the analyst launches eFAST™ Software, scans the directories, and

launches only the traces scored as REV to determine if it should pass or fail. The analyst recorded the

number of traces in need of review based on the eFAST™ Software evaluation. HQ (high quality) traces

were accepted as passing without review and LQ (low quality) traces were accepted as failing without

review. All 344 traces were assessed in this manner and the entire process was timed.

A one-sided, two-sample *t*-test for equality of means, assuming unequal variances[1], was used to

assess if the time required to complete the screening using Method 1 is significantly greater than the

time required to complete the screening using Method 2. In addition to the time study, the accuracy of

the automated filtering method using eFAST™ Software was assessed. The following were counted: 1)

the number of traces that failed the metrics but would have passed with an analyst's review, or false

---

[1] Equality of variances was assessed using an F-test (F = 11.46; p= 0.038); based on the results, unequal
variances were assumed for the two-sample *t*-test.

NIJ Cooperative Agreement 2008-DNA-BX-K192

negatives; and, 2) the number of traces that passed the metrics but failed with an analyst's review, or false positives.

Results

Sample Set	Analyst	Time using Method 1 minutes	Time using Method 2 minutes	Time Savings minutes (% decrease)
Batch 4 R1 (n = 86)	1	20	3	17 (85%)
Batch 6 R1 (n = 86)	2	38	8	30 (79%)
Batch 4 A4 (n = 86)	1	20	3	17 (85%)
Batch 6 A4 (n = 86)	2	15	1	14 (93%)
	Totals	93	15	78 (84%)

Table 3. Time study results comparing Method 1 to Method 2. The times required for analysis under Method 1 and Method 2 were recorded. The percent decrease was calculated by dividing the time savings (in minutes) by the time required under Method 1.

	*Mean time for 86 traces (one plate)	Standard Deviation	Standard Error
Method 1	23.25	10.11	5.06
Method 2	3.75	2.99	1.49
Difference	19.50	7.13	3.57

Table 4. Descriptive statistics for the four sample sets. The mean, standard deviation, and standard error were calculated for the four sample sets used in this time trial. All units are in minutes. *The results of the one-sided, two sample t-test indicate that the mean time required to process 86 traces using Method 1 is significantly greater than that using Method 2 ($n_1 = n_2 = 4$; $P = 0.01$).

NIJ Cooperative Agreement 2008-DNA-BX-K192

	Batch 4 R1 (n = 86)	Batch 6 R1 (n = 86)	Batch 4 A4 (n = 86)	Batch 6 A4 (n = 86)	Totals (n = 344)	Percent
Number of traces scored HQ	55	53	70	81	259	75.29%
Number of traces scored REV	26	33	13	5	77	22.38%
Number of traces scored LQ	5	0	3	0	8	2.33%
Number of FPs	2	2	3	6	13	3.78%
Number of FNs	0	0	0	0	0	0.00%
Number of traces correctly sorted automatically $[(HQ +LQ) - (FP + FN)]$	58	51	70	75	254	73.83%

Table 5. Accuracy of eFAST™ Software assessment of sequence traces. The results of automated sorting were compared to the classification made by the analyst when each trace was assessed manually. Instances of false negative and false positive rates were tabulated. HQ = high quality; REV = review; LQ = low quality; FP = false positive, the number of traces failed by the analyst but scored HQ by eFAST™ sorting criteria; FN = false negative, the number of traces passed by the analyst but scored LQ by eFAST™ sorting criteria.

Discussion and Conclusion

The time study results indicate a significant increase in efficiency when using eFAST™ Software (Method 2) to screen the sequence traces for quality (p = 0.01; Tables 3 and 4). Approximately 74% of the 344 traces were correctly assessed as high quality or low quality without requiring any intervention from the analyst. The false positive rate (Table 5) observed using Method 2 was further investigated. All 13 of the traces were called as low quality by the analyst due to high baseline, but were scored as HQ by eFAST™ Software. Conversations with the eFAST™ Software programmers revealed that the base calling algorithm (TraceTuner™, Paracel, Inc., Pasadena, CA) does not weight baseline noise as heavily in the QV algorithm as other basecalling programs previously used. Since the QVs are subsequently used to determine trace score and trace trimming, the difference in peak scoring algorithm causes differences in the efficiency of trace filtering based on the current metrics. While this error rate is low, there is opportunity to further enhance the sorting capabilities of eFAST™ Software. Additionally, the number of REV traces for the R1 primer data set is higher than for the A4 primer data set. This difference is due to the fact that the REV margin for traces that sequence into a homopolymeric stretch (as is the case with R1 traces) or length heteroplasmic stretch must be wider in order to prevent such traces from failing (Figure 23). Consequently, more traces require analyst review which decreases the efficiency of eFAST™ Software for sorting such traces. For these reasons, additional rules have been programmed into eFAST™ Software v.2.0 in order to reduce the error rate of this process.

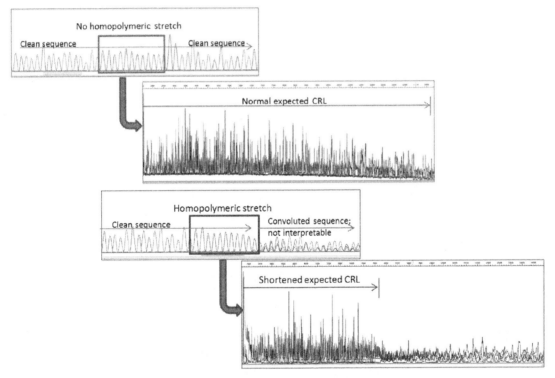

Figure 23. Primer specific trace anomalies. Primer R1 is a representative primer that sequences into a region that occasionally contains a homopolymeric stretch. Shown here is the HV1 homopolymeric site for two individuals, one without a homopolymeric stretch (top pane) and one with a homopolymeric stretch (bottom pane). If an individual does not have a thymine to "anchor" this region, strand slippage occurs and convoluted data results. Such traces are interpretable up to this point and should not fail; therefore, the CRL requirement review range (REV) must be widened.

eFAST™ Software v2.0

Seven new expert system rules (in addition to TS and CRL) are featured in eFAST™ Software v2.0 in order to further enhance the efficiency and discriminatory power of the sorting algorithms (Table 6). They include High Baseline (HB), High Signal (HS), Low Signal (LS), Partial Read (PR), Mixture (Mix), Homopolymeric Stretch (HPS), and Length Heteroplasmy (LH). These additional rules decrease the error rate seen in eFAST™ Software v1.1 and provide valuable insight into trace nuances. The Trace Summary table has been expanded to incorporate the rules, where symbolic flags are used to indicate the status of each rule (Figure 24). A green check indicates that the trace passes the rule and does not exhibit the rule characteristic. A yellow exclamation point indicates that the trace may exhibit the characteristic being tested. A red X indicates that the trace does exhibit the rule characteristic. Certain rule conditions will not be detectable if another rule has previously fired. Such instances are indicated by "NC", not checked.

Rule Name	Type of Rule	Description
High Baseline	Enforced	Nested minor peaks in the primary signal (user defined)
High Signal	Informative	Signal intensity saturates the CCD camera; potential pull up peaks
Low Signal	Enforced (if defined)	Average signal intensity below a threshold (user defined)
Partial Read	Informative	Peaks suddenly decrease in intensity and change in morphology; potentially fixed by reinjection
Mixture	Informative	An observed number of high quality mixed bases observed in the trimmed trace (user defined)
Homopolymeric Stretch	Enforced	A series of homogenous bases followed by an increase in baseline noise; creates a CRL exception
Length Heteroplasmy	Enforced	A heteroplasmic insertion/deletion causing out-of-phase minor species peaks; creates a CRL exception

Table 6. Description of additional rules and functionality.

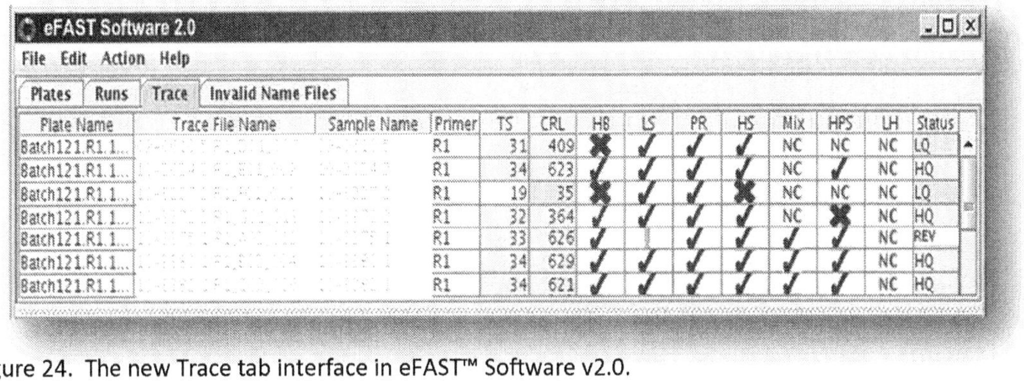

Figure 24. The new Trace tab interface in eFAST™ Software v2.0.

The rules are either *informative*, in which it simply alerts the analyst of a condition, or *enforced,* in which the rule status affects the overall status of the trace. *Informative* rules guide the analyst in further action; for example, the PR rule indicates that an electrophoretic issue occurred, causing a sudden loss of signal (Figure 25). A PR trace usually fails the CRL and/or TS rule(s), but since this anomaly is easily remedied by reinjection, it is very beneficial for the analyst to be informed of the condition. In contrast to the PR rule, the HPS rule is an example of an *enforced* rule; it indicates that a homopolymeric stretch has been detected in the trace. When this occurs, as discussed previously with regard to R1 traces, the expected CRL is truncated. With HPS detected, the CRL rule firing will be overridden and affects the overall status of the trace.

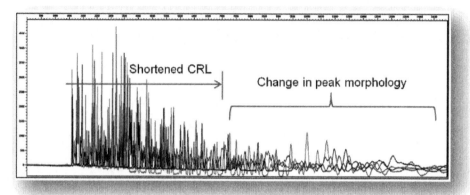

Figure 25. The PR rule firing. This is an example of an informative rule. This trace would fail due to shortened CRL and/or poor TS. However, since this condition is remedied by reinjection, the rule firing informs the analyst to consider reinjecting the trace.

Conclusion

Using eFAST™ Software v1.1 significantly decreases the time required to assess sequence trace quality. Although there is an error rate associated with the trace sorting algorithm used in eFAST™ Software v1.1, this approach has great potential to increase automation and objectivity in the process of screening traces for quality.

While version 1.1 demonstrates significant efficiency improvement, there were opportunities for further development. eFAST™ Software v2.0 introduces an approach to sequence data quality assessment that is entirely novel. The expert system rules incorporated into eFAST™ Software v2.0 are currently being optimized and evaluated for performance and efficiency improvement (NIJ Award 2009-DN-BX-K171).

Robotics

Different robotic platforms were considered for increasing efficiency of mtDNA laboratory processing. Robotic liquid handling techniques can help ensure consistency in pipetting and increase throughput capabilities in a laboratory. The Tecan Freedom EVO® 200 robot (Tecan Group Ltd.) using an 8-fixed-tip LiHa (Liquid Handling arm), a RoMa (Robotic Manipulator arm), and a 96 MCA (MultiChannel Arm) was purchased and validated for high throughput processing for both pre-PCR and post-PCR procedures. Many studies were conducted to optimize liquid classes, identify the best process for moving plates, and create the most efficient program. After these studies were finalized, a thorough evaluation was performed to evaluate the effectiveness of the robotics in relation to time-savings, improved quality control (*i.e.,* no sample switches), quality of data generated using the FTD validated procedures, and profiles reported as compared to the methods used by the FRS section.

Overall Validation Study: Tecan Freedom EVO® 200

The extracted DNA from three batches previously processed by the FRS section was evaluated. Each plate of extracted DNA contained samples for both nDNA and mtDNA analysis. The focus of this study was to process the same batch extracts for mtDNA using the procedures previously described on the robotics platform. Since no cherry-picking features are available, FTD processed all samples on the plate for mtDNA analysis. The FRS section only processed those samples requiring mtDNA analysis, *e.g.,* maternal relatives. These samples were processed according to FRS section's standard procedure, using robotics only for extraction. FTD processed the mtDNA samples using the proposed high throughput robotic methods. The methods performed on the Tecan Freedom EVO® 200 included reduced reaction quantification, normalization of DNA extract, mtDNA amplification setup of the large amplicon, mtDNA post-amplification purification, and cycle sequencing setup for four primers. The batches were then manually setup for XTerminator™ purification. All sequence data obtained from the samples using both the FRS process and the FTD validated process were then compared.

mtDNA Analysis

The three batches had a total of 111 family reference samples for mtDNA analysis. Table 7 presents a summary of the total number of samples processed and the total number of concordant results between the FRS section and the proposed procedures by FTD. Seven samples produced no results by FTD. Table 8 presents the average number of bases reported by the two different procedures.

111	Total Samples
104	Concordant
7	No results obtained by FTD

Table 7. Summary table of samples compared and concordant. Two of the failed samples had low amounts of DNA in the quantification results and one sample had no amount of amplifiable DNA. The other four samples produced sufficient quantification results; however, failed to produce sequence data. The four samples that failed to produce results were subjected to robotic pipetting of one microliter.

Average Number of Bases	
722	FRS
990	FTD

Table 8. The average number of bases reported by the FRS section when performing two separate amplifications for HV1 and HV2 is less than the average number of bases reported by FTD since the new amplification procedure amplifies a larger fragment; an average of 268 bases of additional information is gathered by FTD.

Reported Heteroplasmy			
Sample	rCRS Position	FRS	FTD
08-7384.3	214A	R	R
10-3017.1	16,311T	Y	Y
10-3037.2	214A	R	A
10-3055.1	16,093T	Y	C
	234A	R	A
10-3185.1	16,325T	Y	Y
10-3186.1	228G	R	G
10-3203.2	16,192C	Y	T
10-3391.1	16,189T	Y	Y
10-3440.1	16,093T	Y	Y
10-3460.1	16,093T	Y	Y
10-3546.1	16,093T	Y	C
10-3566.1	195T	Y	Y
10-3577.1	16,093T	Y	Y
10-3578.1	16,093T	Y	Y
10-3611.1	16,093T	Y	Y

Table 9. Summary table of reported heteroplasmy by the FRS section using dRhodamine chemistry and FTD using BigDye Terminator v1.1. Heteroplasmic calls were attributed to analyst subjectivity and noted differences in the signal from the chemistry.

Amplification	FRS	FTD
Initial HV1 Amplification	111	-
Initial HV2 Amplification	111	-
Initial Large Amplicon Amplification	-	244
Total	**222**	**244**

Table 10. Summary table of the total number of amplifications performed for three batches of samples. The FRS section performs two amplifications for each sample and manually cherry picks the samples to be amplified that are needed for maternal familial relationships. FTD performs a single amplification for each sample; since FTD operates in a high throughput mode, all samples on the plate were amplified for mtDNA resulting in additional amplifications. For the three batches compared, 133 additional samples were processed by FTD.

NIJ Cooperative Agreement 2008-DNA-BX-K192

Reamplifications	FRS	FTD
HV1	14[a]	-
HV2	68[b]	-
Large Amplicon (HV1 and HV2)	-	62[b]
Total	**82**	**62**

Table 11. Summary table of reamplifications performed by FRS and FTD.

Resequencing	FRS	FTD
A1	12[a]	-
R1	-	1[a]
B1	8[a],2[d]	-
C1	68[b]	62[b]
D1	68[b]	-
R2	-	62[b]
D2	2[d]	-
D3Y	-	5[a]
A4	18[c]	24[c]
B4	16[c]	24[c]
Total	**194**	**178**

Table 12. Summary table of samples requiring resequencing by FRS and FTD.

[a]Five samples were reamplified for HV1 by the FRS section due to a G to A transition at position 16,390 in HV1. The variant was identified in initial sequencing data from primer A1; however, to achieve confirmation, the FRS section must reamplify HV1. In contrast, FTD amplifies the large amplicon; therefore, the reverse primer D3Y can be used to confirm the 16,390 transition; a savings of five amplifications was achieved by FTD. One sample was reamplified because of a homopolymeric stretch in HV1 and a variant was present in the primer binding site of primer A4. Additionally, due to analyst discretion, eight samples were reamplified by FRS because of a homopolymeric stretch in HV1.

[b]68 HV2 reamplifications were prepared by the FRS section and 62 large amplicon amplifications were prepared by FTD. These samples contained length heteroplasmy in HV2 and required amplification to obtain confirmation. Because one sample also needed to be reamplified for the HV1 region, FTD did not need to amplify the sample for HV2. Additionally, due to human error, five samples were incorrectly amplified by the FRS section.

[c]24 samples had a homopolymeric stretch in HV1 and required re-sequencing of these regions with primers A4 and B4 by FTD. 16 of these samples had a homopolymeric stretch in HV1 and required re-sequencing of these regions with primers A4 and B4 by the FRS section. In addition, due to analyst discretion, the remaining eight samples were reamplified for confirmation. The two additional resequencing reactions performed with primer A4 were to confirm the present of a 16,390A transition.

[d]One sample was resequenced by the FRS section with primer D2 due to noisy baseline. The three additional sequencing reactions were mistakenly performed.

NIJ Cooperative Agreement 2008-DNA-BX-K192

Cost Analysis

AMPLIFICATION

FTD	Kit Price	Cost/μL	Amount(μL)/Reaction	Cost/Reaction		Batch of 86 samples
AmpliTaq Gold (10-tubes)	$1,846.00	$3.08	0.6	$1.85		$158.76

FRS	Kit Price	Cost/μL	Amount(μL)/2 Reactions	Cost/2 Reactions		Batch of 86 samples
AmpliTaq Gold (10-tubes)	$1,846.00	$3.08	1	$3.08		$264.59

Total savings/batch	25 Batches/yr
$105.84	$2,645.93

Table 13. A savings of $1.23 ($3.08 cost per reaction by FRS - $1.85 cost per reaction by the FTD section) per sample was calculated for amplification if the FTD procedures were implemented.

POST-AMPLIFICATION PROCESSING

FTD	Kit Price	Cost/μL	Amount(μL)/Reaction	Cost/Reaction	Cost/Sample (x4 primers)	Batch of 86 samples
ExoSAP-IT (1mL)	$377.00	$0.38	2	$0.75	$0.75	$64.84
BigDye 1.1 (8mL, 8000 reduced rxns)	$8,500.00	$1.06	1	$1.06	$4.25	$365.50
BetterBuffer (10-0.5mL tubes)	$368.00	$0.12	5	$0.61	$2.45	$210.99
XTerminator (20mL kit, 4000rxns)	$1,830.00	$0.09	5	$0.46	$1.83	$157.38
					$9.29	$798.71

FRS	Kit Price	Cost/μL	Amount(μL)/Reaction	Cost/Reaction	Cost/Sample (x4 primers)	Batch of 86 samples
ExoSAP-IT (1mL)	$377.00	$0.38	10	$3.77	$3.77	$324.22
dRhodamine	$7,380.00	$0.92	8	$7.38	$29.52	$2,538.72
Performa® DTR Ultra 96-well Plates	$55.90	-	-	$0.58	$2.33	$223.60
					$35.62	$3,086.54

Total savings/batch	25 Batches/yr
$2,287.83	$57,195.73

Table 14. A savings of $26.33 per sample ($35.62 per sample for FRS - $9.29 per sample for FTD) was calculated for post-amplification procedures.
NOTE: The cost per reaction is a conservative estimate. If only one sample is processed, a Performa® DTR Gel Filtration Cartridge (a single tube device as opposed to a plate) may be used by the FRS section and would cost $1.81 per reaction instead of $0.58 per reaction thus increasing the total cost per reaction.

Total Savings Per Sample*	$27.56
Total Savings Per Batch	$2,393.67
Total Savings Per Year	$59,841.67

Table 15. Average calculated savings (Amplification at $1.23 per sample and Post Amplification Processing at $26.33 per sample added together) using the methods developed "per sample", "per batch," and "per year" with the number of samples received and tested in 2010.
NOTE: *The total savings per sample represents the savings when sequencing four primers per sample using the most conservative estimates.

Conclusion

The FTD has presented several steps in the analysis of mtDNA for reference samples that significantly reduces labor in both the laboratory and in data analysis, reduces the reagent costs, and reduces the overall analytical time. A reduction in labor, reagents, and processing time will improve efficiency and increase the overall capacity of mtDNA processing by the laboratory. With increased efficiency and capacity, more reference samples can be processed and hence, identifications can be recommended earlier.

The quality of the data generated by the presented procedures is occasionally of a lesser quality than the data generated by the dRhodamine procedure used by the FRS section; however, considering the cost savings, time savings, 100% concordance of reported mtDNA haplotypes, and lack of human intervention in many steps, the procedures reported are recommended.

Considerable savings in costs and time can be achieved by implementing these procedures. The FTD and the FRS section have worked closely with The Urban Institute to document the time to process the three batches; the timings to perform all of the procedures both manually and robotically have been documented for numerous steps. The Urban institute will issue an accounting at the conclusion of its study to report any time-savings achieved through the presented procedures using the chemistry, software, and robotic systems.

The total savings per sample when sequencing four primers is $27.56. Implementation of high throughput robotics allows the analysts to focus on data review and the bottleneck presented by sequence data analysis. Further optimization of extremely small volume liquid classes could potentially prevent some of the sample failures observed by FTD.

References

Andrews, R. M., Kubacka, I., Chinnery, P. F., Lightowlers, R. N., Turnbull, D. M., & Howell, N. (1999) Reanalysis and revision of the Cambridge Reference Sequence for human mitochondrial DNA. *Nature Genetics, 23*(2), 147. doi:10.1038/13779

Applied Biosystems (2002) BigDye® Terminator v3.1 and v1.1 cycle sequencing kits product bulletin, Foster City, CA.

Applied Biosystems (2006) BigDye® XTerminator™ purification kit protocol summary, Foster City, CA.

Bell, J. (2008) A simple way to treat PCR products prior to sequencing using ExoSAP-IT®. *BioTechniques, 44*(6), 834.

Curtis, P. C., Thomas, J. L., Phillips, N. R., & Roby, R. K. (2010) Optimization of primer-specific filter metrics for the assessment of mitochondrial DNA sequence data. *Mitochondrial DNA, 21*(6), 191-191-197. doi:10.3109/19401736.2010.528756

Federal Bureau of Investigation (2009) Quality assurance standards for forensic DNA testing laboratories and quality assurance standards for convicted offender DNA databasing laboratories. *Forensic Science Communications, 2*(3).

Gel Company. Better Sequencing Better Reads: BetterBuffer brochure, San Francisco, CA.

Holland, M. M., Fisher, D. L., Roby, R. K., Ruderman, J., Bryson, C., & Weedn, V. W. (1995) Mitochondrial DNA sequence analysis of human remains. *Crime Laboratory Digest, 22*(4), 108-115.

International Organization for Standardization. (2005) ISO/IEC 17025:2005 general requirements for the competence of testing and calibration laboratories.

Isenberg, A. R. (2004) Forensic mitochondrial DNA analysis. In R. Saferstein (Ed.), *Forensic science handbook, Volume II* (Second Edition ed., pp. 297-327). Upper Saddle River, NJ: Prentice-Hall.

Kavlick, M. F., Lawrence, H. S., Merritt, R. T., Fisher, C., Isenberg, A., Robertson, J. M., & Budowle, B. (In Press) Quantification of human mitochondrial DNA using synthesized DNA standards. *Journal of Forensic Sciences.*

Phillips, N. R., Thomas, J. L., Pantoja, J. A., Gonzalez, S. D., Planz, J. V., Eisenberg, A. J., & Roby, R. K. (2009) *The Chilean population database project: A high throughput approach for DNA profiling of 1000 Chilean population samples. Research Appreciation Day*, Ft. Worth TX.

Roby, R. K., Williamson, P., Josserand, M., Planz, J. V., Lorente, J. A., & Eisenberg, A. J. (2007) Streamlining mitochondrial DNA sequencing of reference samples. *Eighteenth International Symposium on Human Identification*, Hollywood, CA.

Roby, R. K., Thomas, J. L., Phillips, N. R., Gonzalez, S. D., Planz, J. V., & Eisenberg, A. J. (2009) High-throughput processing of mitochondrial DNA analysis using robotics. *Proceedings of the American Academy of Forensic Sciences,* Denver, CO , *15,* 95.

Roby, R. K., Phillips, N. R., Thomas, J. L. , Keppler, R., & Eisenberg, A. J. (2010) Quality assessment and alert messaging software for raw mitochondrial DNA sequence data. *Proceedings of the American Academy of Forensic Sciences,* Seattle, WA *, 16,* 96.

NIJ Cooperative Agreement 2008-DNA-BX-K192

UNT Center for Human Identification
Research & Development Laboratory

Table of Contents

Publications

1. Roby R., Gonzalez S., Phillips N., Planz J., Thomas J., Pantoja Astudillo J., Ge J., Aguirre Morales E., Eisenberg A., Chakraborty R., Bustos P., and Budowle, B. Autosomal STR allele frequencies and Y-STR and mtDNA haplotypes in Chilean sample populations. Forensic Science International: Genetics Supplement Series 2009; 2:532-533.

2. Curtis P., Thomas J., Phillips N., and Roby R. Optimization of primer specific filter metrics for the assessment of mitochondrial DNA sequence data. Mitochondrial DNA. 2010 Dec; 21(6):191-197.

Presentations

1. Roby R. Urban Institute Site Visit. Meeting with The Urban Institute: Fort Worth, TX; February 25, 2009.

2. Roby R., Phillips N., Thomas J., Kepler R., Elling J., and Eisenberg A. Quality Assessment and Alert Messaging Software for Raw Mitochondrial DNA Sequence Data. Conference Proceedings of the Sixteenth American Academy of Forensic Sciences 2010: Seattle, WA; February 25, 2010.

3. Phillips N. eFAST© Software: Automated Quality Assessment, Alert Messaging, File Distribution and Sample Tracking of Mitochondrial DNA Sequence Data. Proceedings of the University of North Texas Health Science Center Eighteenth Annual Research Appreciation Day 2010: Fort Worth, TX; April 23, 2010.

4. Roby R. Improving Efficiency in the (Mitochondrial) DNA Laboratory. The NIJ Conference 2010: Washington, D.C.; June 16, 2010.

5. Phillips N. and Roby, R. Expert System Rules and Software Advancements for Mitochondrial DNA Analysis. Conference Proceedings of the Seventeenth American Academy of Forensic Sciences 2011: Chicago, IL.

Posters

1. Roby R., Thomas J., Phillips N., Gonzalez S., Planz J., and Eisenberg A. High Throughput Processing and Increased Efficiency for Mitochondrial DNA Testing: Robotics, Automated Sample Tracking and Filter Metrics. Poster Presentation at the Fifteenth American Academy of Forensic Science 2009: Denver, CO; February 20, 2009.

UNT Center for Human Identification
Research & Development Laboratory

2. Phillips N., Thomas J., Pantoja J., Gonzalez S., Planz J., Eisenberg A., and Roby R. The Chilean Population Database Project: A High Throughput Approach for DNA Profiling of 1000 Chilean Population Samples. Poster Presentation at the University of North Texas Health Science Center Seventeenth Annual Research Appreciation Day 2009: Fort Worth, TX; March 6, 2009.

3. Gonzalez S., Roby R., Phillips N., Planz J., Thomas J., Pantoja Astudillo J., Ge J., Aquirre Morales E., Eisenberg A., Chakraborty R., Bustos P., and Budowle B. Autosomal STR Allele Frequencies and Y-STR and mtDNA Haplotypes in Chilean Sample Populations. Poster Presentation at the Twenty-Third International Society of Forensic Genetics 2009: Buenos Aires, Argentina; September 16, 2009.

4. Nutall K., Thomas J., Fast S., Shetty P., Vishwanatha J., and Roby R. Prostate Cancer Sample Repository of Sera and DNA. Poster Presentation at the University of North Texas Health Science Center Eighteenth Annual Research Appreciation Day 2010: Fort Worth, TX; April 23, 2010.

5. Sprouse M., Budowle B., and Roby R. Mitochondrial DNA Real-Time Quantitative PCR Assay. Poster Presentation at the University of North Texas Health Science Center Eighteenth Annual Research Appreciation Day 2010: Fort Worth, TX; April 23, 2010.

6. Nutall K., Thomas J., Fast S., Shetty P., Vishwanatha J., and Roby R. Prostate Cancer Sample Repository of Sera and DNA. Poster Presentation at the Fifth Annual Texas Conference on Health Disparities 2010: Fort Worth, TX; May 27, 2010.

7. Thomas J., Phillips N., Eisenberg A., and Roby R. Increasing Efficiency for Mitochondrial DNA Amplification of Reference Samples By Eliminating Time-Consuming and Costly Steps. Poster Presentation at the International Symposium on Human Identification 2010; San Antonio, TX; October 13, 2010.

Relevant Procedures

1. Human DNA Quantification using Reduced Reaction Volume Applied Biosystems Quantifiler® Human DNA Quantification Kit; Research & Development Laboratory

2. Human mtDNA Quantification using a Real-Time qPCR Assay; Research & Development Laboratory

3. Normalization Procedure for Extracted DNA; Research & Development Laboratory, Rev. 1

4. High Throughput Amplifications with the MiniPrep 75 Sample Processor; Research & Development Laboratory, Rev. 2

5. Manual mtDNA Amplification Setup, Rev. 1; Research & Development Laboratory

6. Post-PCR mtDNA Processing; Research & Development Laboratory, Rev. 1

7. mtDNA Sequence Analysis; Research & Development Laboratory

UNT Center for Human Identification
Research & Development Laboratory

Table of Contents

Publications

1. Roby R., Gonzalez S., Phillips N., Planz J., Thomas J., Pantoja Astudillo J., Ge J., Aguirre Morales E., Eisenberg A., Chakraborty R., Bustos P., and Budowle, B. Autosomal STR allele frequencies and Y-STR and mtDNA haplotypes in Chilean sample populations. Forensic Science International: Genetics Supplement Series 2009; 2:532-533.

2. Curtis P., Thomas J., Phillips N., and Roby R. Optimization of primer specific filter metrics for the assessment of mitochondrial DNA sequence data. Mitochondrial DNA. 2010 Dec; 21(6):191-197.

Presentations

1. Roby R. Urban Institute Site Visit. Meeting with The Urban Institute: Fort Worth, TX; February 25, 2009.

2. Roby R., Phillips N., Thomas J., Kepler R., Elling J., and Eisenberg A. Quality Assessment and Alert Messaging Software for Raw Mitochondrial DNA Sequence Data. Conference Proceedings of the Sixteenth American Academy of Forensic Sciences 2010: Seattle, WA; February 25, 2010.

3. Phillips N. eFAST© Software: Automated Quality Assessment, Alert Messaging, File Distribution and Sample Tracking of Mitochondrial DNA Sequence Data. Proceedings of the University of North Texas Health Science Center Eighteenth Annual Research Appreciation Day 2010: Fort Worth, TX; April 23, 2010.

4. Roby R. Improving Efficiency in the (Mitochondrial) DNA Laboratory. The NIJ Conference 2010: Washington, D.C.; June 16, 2010.

5. Phillips N. and Roby, R. Expert System Rules and Software Advancements for Mitochondrial DNA Analysis. Conference Proceedings of the Seventeenth American Academy of Forensic Sciences 2011: Chicago, IL.

Posters

1. Roby R., Thomas J., Phillips N., Gonzalez S., Planz J., and Eisenberg A. High Throughput Processing and Increased Efficiency for Mitochondrial DNA Testing: Robotics, Automated Sample Tracking and Filter Metrics. Poster Presentation at the Fifteenth American Academy of Forensic Science 2009: Denver, CO; February 20, 2009.

UNT Center for Human Identification
Research & Development Laboratory

2. Phillips N., Thomas J., Pantoja J., Gonzalez S., Planz J., Eisenberg A., and Roby R. The Chilean Population Database Project: A High Throughput Approach for DNA Profiling of 1000 Chilean Population Samples. Poster Presentation at the University of North Texas Health Science Center Seventeenth Annual Research Appreciation Day 2009: Fort Worth, TX; March 6, 2009.

3. Gonzalez S., Roby R., Phillips N., Planz J., Thomas J., Pantoja Astudillo J., Ge J., Aquirre Morales E., Eisenberg A., Chakraborty R., Bustos P., and Budowle B. Autosomal STR Allele Frequencies and Y-STR and mtDNA Haplotypes in Chilean Sample Populations. Poster Presentation at the Twenty-Third International Society of Forensic Genetics 2009: Buenos Aires, Argentina; September 16, 2009.

4. Nutall K., Thomas J., Fast S., Shetty P., Vishwanatha J., and Roby R. Prostate Cancer Sample Repository of Sera and DNA. Poster Presentation at the University of North Texas Health Science Center Eighteenth Annual Research Appreciation Day 2010: Fort Worth, TX; April 23, 2010.

5. Sprouse M., Budowle B., and Roby R. Mitochondrial DNA Real-Time Quantitative PCR Assay. Poster Presentation at the University of North Texas Health Science Center Eighteenth Annual Research Appreciation Day 2010: Fort Worth, TX; April 23, 2010.

6. Nutall K., Thomas J., Fast S., Shetty P., Vishwanatha J., and Roby R. Prostate Cancer Sample Repository of Sera and DNA. Poster Presentation at the Fifth Annual Texas Conference on Health Disparities 2010: Fort Worth, TX; May 27, 2010.

7. Thomas J., Phillips N., Eisenberg A., and Roby R. Increasing Efficiency for Mitochondrial DNA Amplification of Reference Samples By Eliminating Time-Consuming and Costly Steps. Poster Presentation at the International Symposium on Human Identification 2010; San Antonio, TX; October 13, 2010.

Forensic Science International: Genetics Supplement Series 2 (2009) 532–533

Contents lists available at ScienceDirect

Forensic Science International: Genetics Supplement Series

journal homepage: www.elsevier.com/locate/FSIGSS

Research article

Autosomal STR allele frequencies and Y-STR and mtDNA haplotypes in Chilean sample populations

Rhonda K. Roby [a,*], Suzanne D. Gonzalez [a], Nicole R. Phillips [a], John V. Planz [a], Jennifer L. Thomas [a], Jaime A. Pantoja Astudillo [b], Jianye Ge [a], Eugenia Aguirre Morales [b], Arthur J. Eisenberg [a], Ranajit Chakraborty [c], Patricio Bustos [b], Bruce Budowle [a]

[a] University of North Texas Health Science Center, Ft. Worth, TX, United States
[b] Servicio Médico Legal, Ministerio de Justicia, Gobierno de Chile, Santiago, Chile
[c] University of Cincinnati, Cincinnati, OH, United States

ARTICLE INFO

Article history:
Received 29 August 2009
Accepted 2 September 2009

Keywords:
Chilean population
Hardy–Weinberg equilibrium
Haplotype diversity
Autosomal STRs
Y-STRs
mtDNA

ABSTRACT

DNA from 1020 unrelated male individuals sampled from five locations of Chile (Iquique, Santiago, Concepción, Temuco, and Punta Arenas) were typed for autosomal STRs, Y-STRs, and the mtDNA Control Region. The populations were selected to develop reference databases to support forensic casework and relationship testing. Allele frequencies for 15 autosomal STR loci across the five sampled sites were compiled. As there was considerable overlapping of birthplaces of subjects sampled from these five sites, the pooled dataset was re-grouped based on birthplaces of the subjects into eight geo-political birthplace regions of the country. Each of these populations was evaluated for conformance to Hardy–Weinberg equilibrium (HWE) and linkage disequilibrium (LD) between loci and within the populations was assessed. Descriptive statistics, i.e., power of discrimination (PD), power of exclusion (PE), and mean power of exclusion were determined. No deviations from HWE expectations ($p < 0.05$) and LD were detected. Combined PD and PE for each population exceeded 0.99999. Y-STR and mtDNA haplotype frequencies were developed and haplotype sharing within and between populations was evaluated. The PD for the Y-STR database is 0.99841 and for the mtDNA database it is 0.99356. Population substructure on the haplotype data evaluated by AMOVA indicated approximately 0.03% of the variation detected originated from differences among the eight birthplace regions. Independence between Y-STR haplotypes, mtDNA haplotypes, and autosomal loci was assessed using a mismatch distribution approach.

© 2009 Published by Elsevier Ireland Ltd.

1. Introduction

A population database for the country of Chile was developed using three genotyping systems: autosomal STRs (Table 1), Y-STRs (DYS19, DYS385a/b, DYS389I, DYS389II, DYS390, DYS391, DYS392, DYS393, DYS437, DYS438, DYS439, DYS448, DYS456, DYS458, DYS635, Y-GATA-H4), and mtDNA sequences encompassing HV1 and HV2. The database was developed to assess the significance of potential genetic associations.

2. Materials and methods

A total of 1020 buccal swabs were collected from male individuals in five different locations of the country from north to south: Iquique, Santiago, Concepción, Temuco, and Punta Arenas. The birthplaces of the individuals were noted at the time of collection in order to examine the demographic heterogeneity within the sampling sites.

DNA was extracted using the DNA IQ™ System (Promega Corporation, Madison, USA) on the Tecan Freedom EVO® 100 (Tecan Group Ltd., Männedorf, Switzerland) [1]. The STR loci were genotyped with the AmpFLSTR® Identifiler® [2] and Yfiler® PCR Amplification Kits [3] (Applied Biosystems, Foster City, USA). The mtDNA was sequenced using BigDye® Terminator v.1.1 Cycle Sequencing Kit (Applied Biosystems). All samples were subjected to electrophoresis on the ABI Prism® 3130xl Genetic Analyzer (Applied Biosystems).

Allele frequencies for 15 autosomal STR loci were calculated based on five collection localities, eight birthplace groupings, and total population. Autosomal STR data were tested for deviation from Hardy–Weinberg equilibrium (HWE) and linkage equilibrium expectations using permutation-based empirical tests. A STRUC-TURE analysis was performed. F_{ST}, PD (power of discrimination), PE (power of exclusion), and related statistics were evaluated to study

* Corresponding author at: University of North Texas Health Science Center, Department of Forensic & Investigative Genetics, 3500 Camp Bowie Boulevard, Room 310, Ft. Worth, TX 76107, USA. Tel.: +1 817 735 2462; fax: +1 817 735 5016.
E-mail address: rroby@hsc.unt.edu (R.K. Roby).

1875-1768/$ – see front matter © 2009 Published by Elsevier Ireland Ltd.
doi:10.1016/j.fsigss.2009.09.010

Table 1
Descriptive statistics of autosomal STR loci.

Locus	No. of alleles	Range (repeat units)	$H_{obs.}$	$H_{exp.}$	p-Value	PD	PE	Mean PE Def	Mean PE Trio
CSF1PO	12	6.3–15	0.74138	0.72846	0.11178	0.87453	0.92627	0.31146	0.48356
D2S1338	13	15–27	0.85091	0.85950	0.36243	0.96540	0.98026	0.56162	0.72131
D3S1358	10	11–20	0.74341	0.74459	0.14373	0.89565	0.93476	0.34452	0.52268
D5S818	8	7–14	0.70690	0.70919	0.06061	0.87609	0.91543	0.30811	0.48564
D7S820	10	7–15	0.77688	0.76357	0.62715	0.90667	0.94410	0.37197	0.55012
D8S1179	10	8–17	0.80426	0.80083	0.73492	0.93371	0.96033	0.43981	0.61698
D13S317	8	8–15	0.85903	0.83638	0.10145	0.94982	0.97323	0.50124	0.67207
D16S539	8	8–15	0.78296	0.78734	0.94542	0.92389	0.95477	0.40840	0.58689
D18S51	19	10–27	0.87931	0.87640	0.90622	0.97207	0.98472	0.59875	0.75066
D19S433	17	10.2–18	0.80223	0.80568	0.19817	0.93602	0.96224	0.44930	0.62450
D21S11	20	23.2–35	0.83773	0.83344	0.96281	0.95213	0.97226	0.50492	0.67426
FGA	17	16–29	0.87221	0.87513	0.41810	0.97108	0.98441	0.59397	0.74717
TH01	6	6–10	0.75355	0.77178	0.83834	0.91291	0.94792	0.37607	0.55479
TPOX	10	5–14	0.66836	0.66332	0.69134	0.83216	0.88665	0.25029	0.41496
vWA	10	12–21	0.76471	0.76651	0.26367	0.90918	0.94548	0.37691	0.55591
Total						>0.99999	>0.99999	0.99982	>0.99999

$H_{obs.}$ = observed heterozygosity; $H_{exp.}$ = expected heterozygosity; p-value = p-value of Hardy–Weinberg equilibrium exact test; PD = power of discrimination; PE = power of exclusion; Mean PE Def = PE of deficiency cases; Mean PE Trio = PE of standard trios.

Table 2
Shared Y-STR and mtDNA haplotypes.

Haplotype	Y-STR (N = 978)		mtDNA (N = 1007)	
Counts	Number observed	Frequency	Number observed	Frequency
1	688	0.00102	349	0.000993
2	79	0.00204	63	0.001986
3	22	0.00307	31	0.002979
4	7	0.00409	14	0.003972
5	5	0.00511	10	0.004965
6	1	0.00613	6	0.005958
7	1	0.00716	4	0.006951
8			4	0.007944
9			4	0.008937
10			3	0.00993
11			4	0.010924
12			1	0.011917
13			1	0.01291
15			1	0.014896
16			1	0.015889
29			1	0.028798
42			1	0.041708

the utility of this database for forensic casework and relationship testing.

3. Results and discussion

Individuals sampled in five sites were not necessarily born in geo-political regions close to the sampling sites. Hence, there is overlap in the birthplaces of subjects sampled. In addition, birthplace distribution of individuals across five sampling sites was statistically different from each other. To examine possible genetics heterogeneity in the country, the pooled data were re-grouped according to their birthplaces into eight geo-political regions. In total, 986 full autosomal profiles were obtained. The eight birthplace groups do not show any appreciable differences of allele frequencies at the 15 autosomal STR loci (largest F_{ST} between groups is 0.00445). No deviations from HWE and LD were detected. The number of observed deviations from linkage equilibrium was fewer than would be expected to be observed by chance within each birthplace group and the pooled dataset. A STRUCTURE analysis, supported with the distribution of shared alleles and genotypes between all pairs of individuals, also supports the use of a pooled database for forensic applications in the country. Descriptive statistics of the autosomal STRs are displayed in Table 1.

Y-STR haplotype data from 978 individuals yielded 803 distinct haplotypes with 688 haplotypes observed only once in the total dataset (Table 2). The most common Y-STR haplotype was observed seven times. Comparisons of autosomal profiles of individuals who share the same Y-STR haplotype suggest that some individuals may be biologically related. The F_{ST} based on Y-STR haplotype diversity for the total database is 0.00061 with a corresponding PD of 0.99841. In the sample of 1007 mtDNA profiles, 641 distinct mtDNA haplotypes were observed. The most common mtDNA haplotype was observed 16 times in the population. The F_{ST} of the mtDNA database is 0.003166 with a corresponding PD of 0.99356 for HV1 (i.e., 16024–16365) and HV2 (i.e., 73–340). For the Y-STR and mtDNA haplotypes, the counting method can be used with appropriate correction for sampling error and with a modest level of population substructure adjustment, if necessary.

Analyses of joint distributions of mismatches were performed between all pairs of individuals. Based on autosomal loci, Y-STRs, and mtDNA, these three systems are mutually independent. Statistics with autosomal STR, Y-STR, and mtDNA data may be combined using the product rule as independence of these three systems was demonstrated.

Conflict of interest

None.

Acknowledgments

Dr. Roby would like to acknowledge that techniques and methodologies developed under NIJ Cooperative Agreement 2008-DN-BX-K192, Forensic DNA Unit Efficiency Improvement FY2008, supported the construction of this database.

References

[1] F. Plopper, R. Roby, J. Planz, A. Eisenberg, High throughput processing of family reference samples for missing persons programs: the use of robotics in extraction and amplification setup for STR and mtDNA analysis, in: Conference on the Proceedings of the 17th Intl. Symp. on Human Identification, Nashville, TN, 2006.
[2] P. Collins, L. Hennessy, C. Leibelt, R. Roby, D. Reeder, P. Foxall, Developmental validation of a single-tube amplification of the 13 CODIS STR loci, D2S1338, D19S433 and Amelogenin, J. Forensic Sci. 49 (6) (2004) 1265–1277.
[3] J. Mulero, C. Chang, L. Calandro, R. Green, Y. Li, C. Johnson, L. Hennessy, Development and validation of the AmpFLSTR® Yfiler™ PCR Amplification Kit: a male specific, single amplification 17 Y-STR multiplex system, J. Forensic Sci. 51 (1) (2006) 64–75.

Mitochondrial DNA, December 2010; 21(6): 191–197

informa
healthcare

Optimization of primer-specific filter metrics for the assessment of mitochondrial DNA sequence data

PAMELA C. CURTIS[1], JENNIFER L. THOMAS[1], NICOLE R. PHILLIPS[1], & RHONDA K. ROBY[1,2]

[1]*Department of Forensic and Investigative Genetics, University of North Texas Health Science Center, Fort Worth, TX, USA, and* [2]*Institute of Investigative Genetics, University of North Texas Health Science Center, Fort Worth, TX, USA*

(Received 31 March 2010; revised 20 September 2010; accepted 29 September 2010)

Abstract

Filter metrics are used as a quick assessment of sequence trace files in order to sort data into different categories (i.e. high quality, review, and low quality) without human intervention. The filter metrics consist of two numerical parameters for sequence quality assessment: trace score (TS) and contiguous read length (CRL). Primer-specific settings for the TS and CRL were established using a calibration dataset of 2817 traces and validated using a concordance dataset of 5617 traces. Prior to optimization, 57% of the traces required manual review before import into a sequence analysis program, whereas after optimization only 28% of the traces required manual review. After optimization of primer-specific filter metrics for mitochondrial DNA sequence data, an overall reduction of review of trace files translates into increased throughput of data analysis and decreased time required for manual review.

Keywords: *Filter metrics, expert systems, trace score, contiguous read length, quality assessment*

Introduction

Filter metrics are used as a quick assessment of sequence trace files in order to sort data into different categories (i.e. high quality, review, and low quality) without human intervention (Roby et al. 2009b). Presently, in forensic DNA testing, software tools that use expert system logic are being used to help review single-source nuclear DNA data and to reduce the backlog of convicted offender data for upload into the national DNA database (Roby 2008a). An expert system for nuclear DNA is defined by the forensic community as a software program or set of software programs that identifies peaks/bands, assigns alleles, ensures data meet laboratory-defined criteria, describes rationale behind decisions, and makes no incorrect allele calls without human intervention (Roby and Christen 2007). An expert system applies 'If..., then...' statements to make decisions on the

quality of data and automates allele calling (Hunt 1986; Engelmore and Feigenbaum 1993). The software must provide justification for each decision (Roby and Tincher 2010). Examples of laboratory-defined criteria used for short tandem repeat analysis in GeneMapper™ ID (Applied Biosystems [AB], Foster City, California, USA) include the allele number, peak:height ratio, and off-scale data (Applied Biosystems 2003). The software uses these criteria to quickly signal, or fire a rule, regarding data quality. The rule firings expedite data interpretation through the use of shapes and colors displayed in the user interface of the software. If a sample yields good-quality data and meets all the laboratory-defined thresholds, a green square is displayed for each parameter. If data do not meet a specific laboratory-defined threshold, a rule is fired drawing a scientist's attention to that particular sample or locus via a yellow triangle. A red octagon signifies that a locus or sample failed.

Correspondence: R. K. Roby, Department of Forensic and Investigative Genetics, Institute of Investigative Genetics, University of North Texas Health Science Center, 3500 Camp Bowie Boulevard, Fort Worth, TX, USA. Tel: + 1 817 735 2462. Fax: + 1 817 735 5016. E-mail: rhonda.roby@unthsc.edu

ISSN 1940-1736 print/ISSN 1940-1744 online © 2010 Informa UK, Ltd.
DOI: 10.3109/19401736.2010.528756

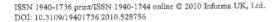

Expert systems have the potential to streamline data analysis and reduce backlogs within laboratories (Perlin et al. 2001; Roby and Jones 2005). An expert system for the sequence analysis should reduce the amount of time a scientist spends reviewing sequence data, and, therefore, should increase sample throughput. A proposed definition for a sequence analysis expert system is a software program or a set of software programs that identifies peaks, assigns bases, ensures data meet laboratory-defined criteria, describes the rationale behind decisions, reviews sequence data prior to use in contigs, reviews the quality of each base, skips to positions of bases with low quality, and searches sequence data for unusual patterns (Roby et al. 2010). Expert systems may also reduce the potential for human error, as the process is automated, consistent, and accurate. Implementation of expert systems within a laboratory reduces analysis time, therefore, freeing the scientist for other duties. No complete expert system for sequence data analysis is presently available. This paper presents an existing software program, Sequence Scanner Software v1.0 (AB), which has rule firings that can assist scientists in the initial review of sequence data.

Software programs are utilized by scientists to build contigs, align trace files, and analyze mitochondrial DNA (mtDNA) sequence data. Prior to analysis of the sequence data, Sequence Scanner Software v1.0 (available at http://www.appliedbiosystems.com) can be used for a quick quality assessment of sequence data. Sequence Scanner Software is a downloadable software program that allows the scientist to display, edit, trim, export, and generate quality assessments of AB BigDye® Terminator sequencing .abl files generated by the suite of ABI PRISM® capillary instrumentation (AB). Within this software program, the scientist can set expert system-like rules and rule firings such as quality value (QV), window size, trace score (TS), and contiguous read length (CRL). QV is a value assigned to each nucleotide (base); the calculation for QV is $-10\log_{10}P_e$, where P_e is the probability of error. A value of 1–60 may be entered for this parameter. The window size is used to calculate the CRL and refers to the first and last stretch of bases with an average QV greater than the laboratory-defined threshold, thus indicating the beginning and end of a CRL. The window size may be set at a value of 5–999. The TS is calculated after trimming the sequence; it is the average of the QVs of all the bases. The CRL is measured by the stretch of bases with a QV greater than or equal to the laboratory-defined threshold. Quality assessments can be made quickly with filter metrics defined by the laboratory as high quality, review, and low quality. With optimized filter metrics, the scientist can quickly assess the quality of sequence files. Data of high quality ('pass') and low quality ('fail') have been characterized within our laboratory and are color-coded with defined thresholds and flagged as green or red, respectively. A yellow flag assigned to a trace file signifies that the data do not fall in the high-quality window nor in the low-quality window and that the scientist should review the data and determine its use in a contig.

Four parameters in Sequence Scanner Software are used as the filter metrics to quickly assess sequence quality (Roby 2008b). Two of these parameters, QV and window size, are held constant whereas two parameters, TS and CRL, are variable. Window size is held constant at 20 bases and QV is held constant at 20 for this study. For example, if a base has a QV = 20, this means it has a $P_e = 1\%$, indicating that there is a 1% chance of being the wrong base call (see Table I). The scientist can set thresholds for TS with color coordination. Prior to optimization of the primer-specific filter metrics, a preliminary evaluation was performed to define these settings. For high-quality data that require no human intervention, high quality is defined as 35–100 for TS. For a low-quality sequence, the TS is defined as 0–20. The review range is defined

Table I.   QV and associated probability of error.

QV	P_e (%)	QV	P_e (%)	QV	P_e (%)	QV	P_e (%)	QV	P_e (%)
1	79	11	7.9	21	0.79	31	0.079	50	0.001
2	63	12	6.3	22	0.63	32	0.063	60	0.0001
3	50	13	5.0	23	0.50	33	0.050	70	0.00001
4	39	14	3.9	24	0.39	34	0.039	80	0.000001
5	31	15	3.1	25	0.31	35	0.031	90	0.0000001
6	25	16	2.5	26	0.25	36	0.025	99	0.00000012
7	20	17	2.0	27	0.20	37	0.020		
8	15	18	1.5	28	0.15	38	0.015		
9	12	19	1.2	29	0.12	39	0.012		
10	10	20	1.0	30	0.10	40	0.010		

Note: Sequence Scanner Software uses the quality per peak, evaluates the overlap of fluorescent signals, and measures a Gaussian fit to determine a peak's QV. QV is a number assigned to each base; $QV = -10\log_{10}P_e$, where P_e is the probability of error. As shown, if a base is assigned a QV of 20, there is a 1% chance of that base call being incorrect. According to Sequence Scanner, high-quality pure bases are generally assigned a QV between 20 and 50. Hence, high QVs indicate a low P_e. For the optimization of primer-specific filter metrics, the QV threshold was held constant at 20. *Source*: Table reproduced from information provided in Sequence Scanner Software v1.0 (Applied Biosystems).

as 21–34. The second parameter assessed is the CRL. The software uses the QV of a single base and adjacent bases that make up a specified window size to calculate the CRL. The CRL also allows the scientist to set thresholds with color coordination. Prior to optimization of the filter metrics, a high-quality sequence was set to be 401 or greater. The low-quality sequence ranged from 0–200. The CRL of sequence traces requiring review was set at 201–400. Prior to this study, these filter metric settings were applied to all sequence data regardless of the individual primer's sequencing read length or location of sequencing primer.

By optimizing the filter metrics defined for each primer, increased throughput of data analysis can be achieved. Furthermore, the scientist can accurately assess the quality of the sequence data without launching or viewing each trace file to determine whether data will be used in the sample's contig. Launching and viewing each trace file is time consuming. The graphic viewer in most software programs allows a display of approximately 50 bases and requires the scientist to scroll through the sequence data. With optimized filter metrics, the scientist no longer needs to launch and view each trace file in order to ascertain the quality of sequence data; he/she only needs to review those sequence traces flagged as 'review'.

Materials and methods

Laboratory processing

The mtDNA sequence data from a population database were used to optimize the filter metrics for this study (Roby et al. 2009a). DNA from 1000 male buccal swabs was extracted using the DNA IQ™ System (Promega Corporation, Madison, Wisconsin, USA) on the Freedom EVO® 100 (Tecan Group, Ltd, Männedorf, Switzerland) (Plopper et al. 2006). A single amplification of a 1.1 kb fragment was performed to generate a sequence that encompasses both hypervariable region 1 (HV1) and hypervariable region 2 (HV2) of the mitochondrial genome (see Figure 1). This single large amplicon was generated using primers R1 (forward) and R2 (reverse). The amplification setup was performed on the MiniPrep 75 Sample Processor (Tecan Group, Ltd). The large amplicon was sequenced using the BigDye® Terminator v1.1 Cycle Sequencing Kit (AB). Cycle sequencing was performed with eight sequencing primers to obtain coverage of the entire amplicon (see Figure 1) (Roby et al. 2008). The PCR products were analyzed via capillary electrophoresis on the ABI PRISM® 3130xl Genetic Analyzer (AB). Prior to aligning and analyzing sequence data, filter metrics (TS = 20, 34 and CRL = 200, 400) are used to assess the sequence trace quality. For the present study, we reviewed each sequence trace and the corresponding sequence quality for each file whenever yellow 'review' flags were fired. The quality of the 'review' sequences was manually

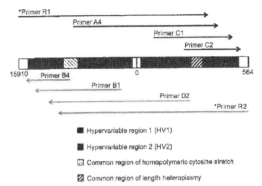

Figure 1. Control region of mtDNA with amplification and cycle sequencing primers. Minimally, forensic laboratories attempt to obtain sequence information from positions 16,024–16,365 (HV1) and positions 73–340 (HV2) in the control region for identification purposes. The dark blue region represents HV1 and the light gray region represents HV2. The green diagonal (\) represents the homopolymeric stretch commonly observed within HV1 and the purple diagonal (/) represents the length heteroplasmy commonly observed within HV2. The white area is the extra information obtained by performing a single large amplification. Black arrows (left to right) indicate forward primers and orange arrows (right to left) indicate reverse primers. Amplification for the 1.1 kb amplicon is performed using *Primer R1 and *Primer R2 of the displacement loop (D-loop) of the mitochondrial genome.

assessed by the following review criteria: baseline noise, signal intensity, read length, and anomalies (e.g. heteroplasmy and homopolymeric stretches). The sequence trace quality was annotated by us on the printed Quality Control Reports, a feature of Sequence Scanner Software. This review was required in order for us to build contigs and to optimize filter metrics.

Optimization of filter metrics

Using the mtDNA sequence trace files and our original notations, we performed optimization of primer-specific filter metrics. Optimization is the process of customizing the filter metrics to improve the accuracy and effectiveness of the filter; verifying that the rule firings are consistent with the human decision-making process; and confirming that the software performs these tasks consistently. The Quality Control Reports generated by Sequence Scanner Software were exported and opened in Microsoft® Excel (Microsoft Corporation, Redmond, Washington, USA). Our comments were manually entered into the Excel spreadsheet. A passing or failing status was assigned to each sequence trace based on review criteria. In order to calibrate the software, a dataset of 2817 sequence trace files was used. Calibration is the process of modifying the filter metrics and determining whether the new settings allow the samples to parse into the appropriate categories; that is, high quality, review, and low quality (Butler 2006; Roby and Christen 2007). A Microsoft® Access (Microsoft Corporation) database

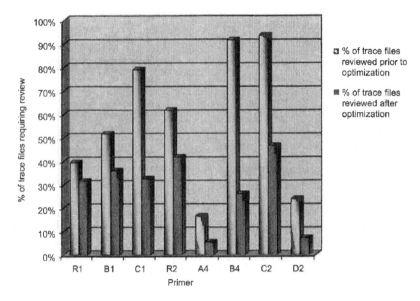

Figure 2.   Percentage of trace files requiring review per primer. The yellow bars (the left most bar for each primer) represent the number of traces requiring manual review prior to filter metric optimization. The blue bars (the right most bar) represent the number of traces requiring review after primer-specific optimization. As can be seen, Primer B4 required more than 90% of the trace files to be manually reviewed prior to optimization. After optimization, less than 30% of the trace files require manual review.

was constructed using the data contained in the Excel spreadsheet for each of the eight primers to allow for quick querying of potential filter metric settings. Concordance was performed to demonstrate that the new filter metrics provided a better assessment of the data than the previous values. A total of 5617 trace files was designated for validation and concordance of the optimized settings. Additional Microsoft® Access databases were constructed for each primer to verify the proposed primer-specific filter metric settings.

Results

Specific filter metrics were defined for each of the eight primers used. After the calibration study, the new filter metrics were applied to the corresponding sequence files. Figure 2 displays the percentage of trace files requiring review prior to optimization and after optimization. As can be seen on this graph, considerable time-savings can be achieved using filter metrics that are optimized per primer (see Figure 2). Since these filter metrics were initially defined using the R1 and R2 primers, which have a long potential read length, optimization of primer-specific filter metrics shows less improvement than that of other primers. Primer-specific filter metrics for B4, C2, and C1 demonstrate a considerable decrease in the number of trace files that would require manual review.

Primer B4 produces a short sequencing fragment of mtDNA (see Figure 1). With optimized filter metrics for Primer B4, 72% of the trace files did not require manual review; these trace files automatically passed.

Table II specifies the breakdown of filter metrics prior to optimization and after optimization for a total of 352 trace files. Prior to optimization, none of the trace files fit into the high-quality category because the CRL threshold was set too high (i.e. CRL = 400) for this short sequencing fragment of approximately 250 bases. After optimization with a CRL set at 200, 222 of the trace files fit into this category and did not require any review prior to use in its contig for sequence analysis. Prior to optimization, 318 trace files were flagged yellow requiring manual review. After optimization, only 97 of the trace files required manual review. The low-quality thresholds were well defined prior to optimization (see Table II). Figure 3 displays a scatterplot of all passing and failing trace files, green and red, respectively, according to our annotations. The green box represents the passing

Table II.   Filter metric assessment for Primer B4.

	Total number of trace files	
Assessment	Before optimization	After optimization
High quality	0	222
Review	318	97
Low quality	34	33
Total	352	352

Note: Prior to optimization, zero trace files had a high-quality filter metric (high-quality TS and high-quality CRL). After optimization, 222 trace files fit into the high-quality category. Prior to optimization, 318 trace files require manual review; and after primer-specific filter metric settings were applied, only 97 trace files required manual review.

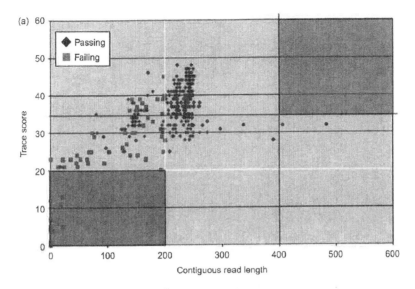

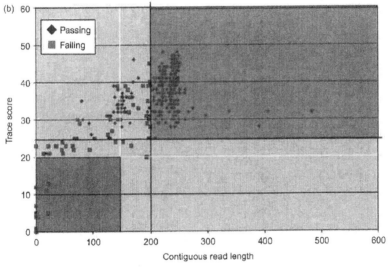

Figure 3.   Scatterplots of Primer B4 filter metrics before and after optimization. The dark green line and the light yellow line on the horizontal axes represent the upper and lower thresholds, respectively, for the TS. The dark green line and the light yellow line on the vertical axes represent the upper and lower thresholds, respectively, for the CRL. Any trace files plotted below both yellow lines in the red box (lower left corner) indicate low-quality data and automatically fail. Any trace files plotted above both green lines in the green box (upper right corner) indicate high-quality data and automatically pass. Each trace file plotted in the middle region requires manual review. (a) Primer B4 trace files prior to primer-specific optimization; no Primer B4 trace files fit into the high-quality category because the thresholds were set too high. (b) Same trace files after primer-specific optimization; high-quality trace files fit into the green box and fewer trace files required manual review after primer-specific optimization of the filter metrics.

filter metrics: passing threshold for TS and passing threshold for CRL. High-quality data should fall in the green box. The red box represents the failing filter metrics: failing threshold for TS and failing threshold for CRL. Low-quality data should fall in the red box. All data in the gray area are subjected to manual review. Figure 3a displays the trace files for Primer B4 prior to primer-specific optimization, and Figure 3b

displays the trace files for the B4 primer after optimization. No trace files fall into the green 'passing' box prior to primer-specific optimization (see Figure 3a). After primer-specific filter metrics are applied, fewer trace files require manual review (see Figure 3b). As illustrated, implementation of primer-specific filter metrics provides an accurate representation of sequence quality and reduces the amount of time a scientist spends reviewing trace files.

Table III.   Primer-specific optimized filter metrics.

Primer	TS			CRL		
	Low quality	Review	High quality	Low quality	Review	High quality
R1	0–20	21–29	30–100	0–200	201–250	≥251
B1	0–20	21–27	28–100	0–150	151–210	≥211
C1	0–20	21–24	25–100	0–150	151–250	≥251
R2	0–20	21–24	25–100	0–110	111–250	≥251
A4	0–20	21–24	25–100	0–200	201–250	≥251
B4	0–20	21–24	25–100	0–150	151–200	≥201
C2	0–20	21–24	25–100	0–100	101–150	≥151
D2	0–20	21–24	25–100	0–100	101–150	≥151

Note: The values are the primer-specific filter metrics for each of the eight sequencing primers defined by our laboratory's internal validation. These values should be used as initial settings for a laboratory. Internal validation should be performed by individual laboratories to define its laboratory-specific settings.

Each of the sequencing primers used has various read length possibilities (see Figure 1). Using the revised Cambridge Reference Sequence, as a reference standard, we counted the number of bases 3′ to the primer binding location (see Figure 1) (Andrews et al. 1999). Primer R1, for example, has a maximum potential read length of 1183 bases; however, if a sequence trace contains an HV1 homopolymeric stretch, the read length is shortened to approximately 253 bases. If a sequence trace does not contain a homopolymeric stretch in HV1 but does contain a length heteroplasmy in HV2, Primer R1 could sequence through HV1 and into HV2 for approximately 941 bases until it reaches the length heteroplasmy in HV2. When sequencing the complementary strand in the reverse direction, Primer R2 has a maximum potential read length of 1183 bases. If a sequence trace contains a length heteroplasmy in HV2, the read length for Primer R2 stops at approximately 230 bases. If Primer R2 is able to sequence through HV2 and into HV1 but stops at approximately 921 bases, an educated assumption can be made that the sequence contains a homopolymeric stretch in HV1. Primer B1 only sequences HV1 and has a maximum potential read length of approximately 460 bases. However, if a B1 sequence trace has a high TS value and a CRL of approximately 198 bases, then that trace file most probably contains a homopolymeric stretch in HV1. Primer C1 only sequences HV2 and has a maximum potential read length of approximately 497 bases. However, if a C1 sequence trace has a high TS value and a CRL of approximately 255, it can be assumed that sequence trace most probably contains a length heteroplasmy in HV2 (see Figure 1).

Optimized filter metrics for the eight sequencing primers used in our laboratory can be found in Table III. Prior to optimization, data from all eight sequencing primers were assessed with TS settings of 20, 34 and CRL settings of 200, 400. Following primer-specific optimization, the TS and CRL settings allow for data to be parsed more consistently based on the primer used for sequencing.

Examples of low-quality, review, and high-quality data for each of the eight sequencing primers can be accessed in the Trace Archive database online (http://www.ncbi.nlm.nih.gov/Traces/home). The TI numbers are as follows: 2281021664, 2281021665, 2281021666, 2281021667, 2281021668, 2281021669, 2281021670, 2281021671, 2281021672, 2281021673, 2281021674, 2281021675, 2281021676, 2281021677, 2281021678, and 2281021679.

Discussion

We have shown that filter metrics are an important tool applied to sequence trace files. By optimizing filter metrics to specific sequencing primers, there was an overall decrease in the number of sequence trace files requiring review. Prior to optimization, we reviewed 57% of the sequence traces. After optimization, only 28% of the sequence traces require manual review. Using defined filter metrics for each primer translates into considerable time-savings. Implementing optimized primer-specific filter metrics yields an estimated time-saving of approximately 50% prior to building a contig. Although humans are prone to error and interruptions, a software program is not and can continuously provide consistent, objective measurements when the software logic is accurate. Increased laboratory throughput has been achieved with optimized filter metrics, with a decrease in analysis times and an increase in consistent assessment of trace files. Future software developments could further automate sequence analysis.

Acknowledgements

The research conducted in this paper was in partial fulfillment of Pamela Musslewhite's (Curtis) master's thesis entitled, 'Optimization of Filter Metrics for mtDNA Sequence Analysis', August 2009. Support for this project was partially funded by NIJ Cooperative Agreement 2008-DN-BX-K192, Forensic DNA Unit Efficiency Improvement, FY 2008.

RIGHTS LINK

Declaration of interest: The authors report no conflicts of interest. The authors alone are responsible for the content and writing of the paper.

References

Andrews RM, Kubacka I, Chinnery PF, Lightowlers RN, Turnbull DM, Howell N. 1999. Reanalysis and revision of the Cambridge reference sequence for human mitochondrial DNA. Nat Genet 23:147.

Applied Biosystems. 2003. GeneMapper™ ID software version 3.1 Human Identification Analysis User Guide. Foster City, California, USA: Applied Biosystems.

Butler J. 2006. Debunking some urban legends surrounding validation within the forensic DNA community. Profiles DNA 9:3–6.

Engelmore RS, Feigenbaum E. 1993. Expert systems and artificial intelligence, available at http://www.wtec.org/loyola/kb/c1_s1.htm (accessed 15 September 2010).

Hunt VD. 1986. Artificial intelligence and expert systems source-book. New York: Chapman and Hall.

Perlin MW, Coffman D, Crouse C, Konotop F, Ban JD. 2001. Automated STR data analysis: Validation studies. In: Twelfth International Symposium on Human Identification – 2001, 29 November. Madison, WI: Promega Corporation.

Plopper F, Roby R, Planz J, Eisenberg A. 2006. High throughput processing of family reference samples for missing persons programs: The use of robotics in extraction and amplification setup for STR and mtDNA analysis. In: Seventeenth International Symposium on Human Identification – 2006, 9–12 October. Nashville, TN: Promega Corporation.

Roby RK. 2008a. Expert systems help labs process DNA samples. Natl Inst Justice J 260:16–19.

Roby RK. 2008b. High throughput mitochondrial DNA analysis: Optimization of sequence chemistry, characterization of

local dye terminator sequencing frames, and tools for the development of an expert system. Doctoral Dissertation, University of Granada, Spain.

Roby RK, Christen AD. 2007. Validating expert systems: Examples with the FSS-i³™ Expert System Software. Profiles DNA 10: 13–15.

Roby RK, Jones JP. 2005. Evaluating expert systems for forensic DNA laboratories, available at http://www3.appliedbiosystems.com/cms/groups/applied_markets_marketing/documents/generaldocuments/cms_042230.pdf (accessed 16 September 2010).

Roby RK, Tincher BM. 2010. Expert systems: High throughput analysis of single source samples for forensic DNA databasing. Report. Huntington, WV: US Department of Justice.

Roby RK, Capt C, Macurdy KM, Planz JV, Lorente JA, Eisenberg AJ. 2008. New tools for mitochondrial DNA sequencing and analysis at the University of North Texas Center for Human Identification Laboratory. In: Proceedings of the American Academy of Forensic Sciences, 18–22 February. Washington, DC.

Roby RK, Gonzalez SD, Phillips NR, Planz JV, Thomas JL, Pantoja Astudillo JA, Ge J, Aguirre Morales E, Eisenberg AJ, Chakraborty R, Bustos P, Budowle B. 2009a. Autosomal STR allele frequencies and Y-STR and mtDNA haplotypes in Chilean sample populations. Forensic Sci Int Genet Suppl Ser 2: 532–533.

Roby RK, Thomas JL, Phillips NR, Gonzalez SD, Planz JV, Eisenberg AJ. 2009b. High-throughput processing of mitochondrial DNA analysis using robotics. In: Proceedings of the American Academy of Forensic Sciences, 16–21 February. Denver, CO.

Roby RK, Phillips NR, Thomas JL, Keppler R, Eisenberg AJ. 2010. Quality assessment and alert messaging software for raw mitochondrial DNA sequence data. In: Proceedings of the American Academy of Forensic Sciences, 22–27 February. Seattle, WA.

Urban Institute Site Visit

FY 2008 Forensic DNA Unit Efficiency Improvement
NIJ Cooperative Agreement 2008-DNA-BX-K192
25 February 2009
Rhonda K. Roby, PhD, MPH
Project Coordinator
Center for Human Identification
Department of Forensic and Investigative Genetics
University of North Texas Health Science Center
Fort Worth, Texas USA

Chemistry

- Single amplicon

Amplification and Sequencing Scheme

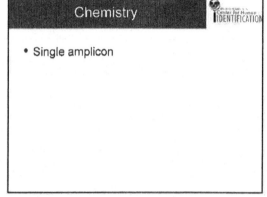

Amplification of Family References

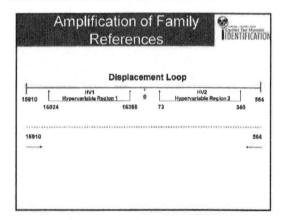

1

Sequencing of Family References

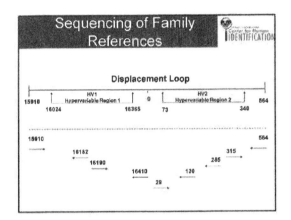

Sample Cleanup – 40 minutes

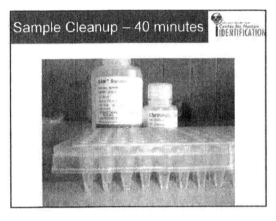

Optimization of Sequence Chemistry

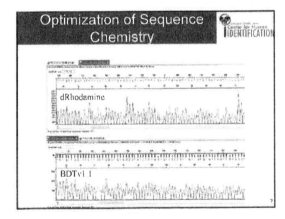

Summary of Chemistry Optimization

- Reduced costs
- Fewer transfers of DNA evidence
- Maintain quality
- Amenable to robotics
- Chemistry available in the future

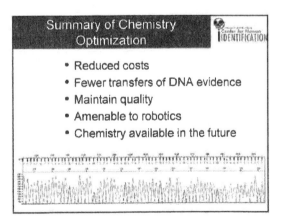

Software

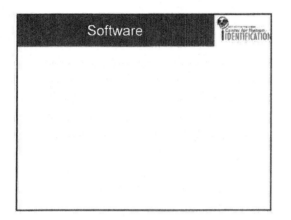

Current Method of Analysis

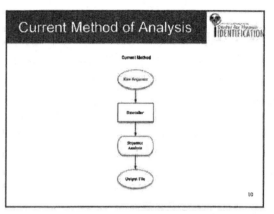

An Expert System is...

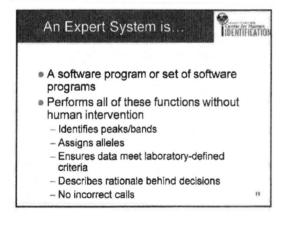

- A software program or set of software programs
- Performs all of these functions without human intervention
  - Identifies peaks/bands
  - Assigns alleles
  - Ensures data meet laboratory-defined criteria
  - Describes rationale behind decisions
  - No incorrect calls

Expert Systems

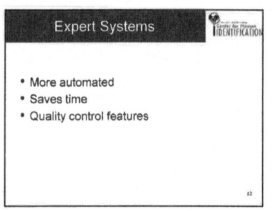

- More automated
- Saves time
- Quality control features

More Automated

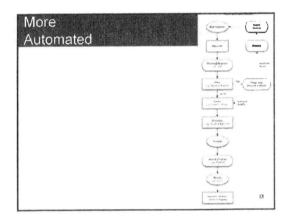

Automated Method

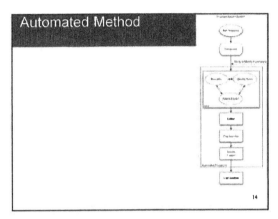

Raw Data and Processed Data

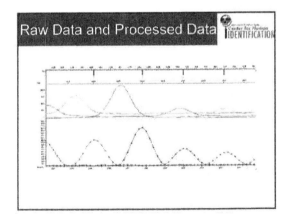

Base Score

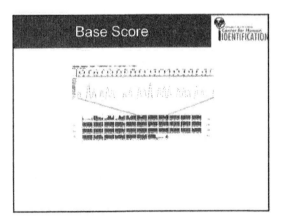

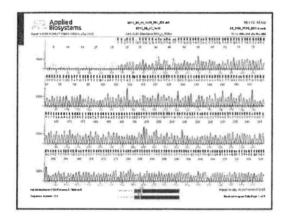

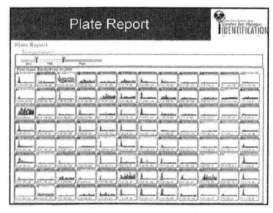

Plate Report

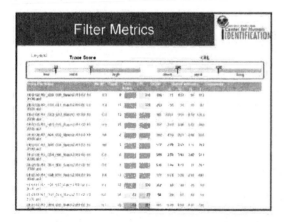

Filter Metrics

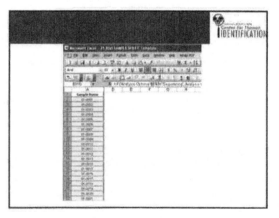

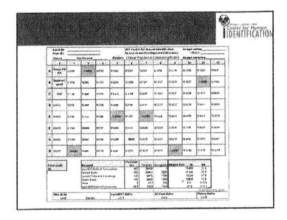

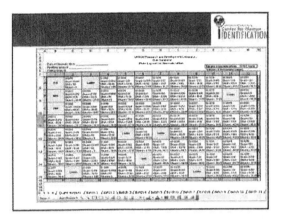

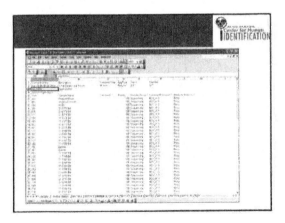

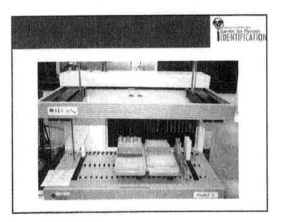

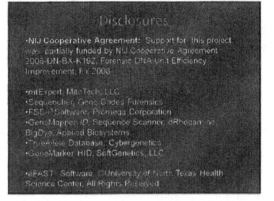

eFAST© Software

- e = expert, electronic, email
- F = Filtering
- A = and Assessment of
- S = Sequence
- T = Traces

eFAST© Software

- Uses numerical information to evaluate and sort data
- Applies expert system rules to evaluate sequence data
- Sends immediate electronic message to analyst
- Does not require review of data to build contigs

Sequence Data

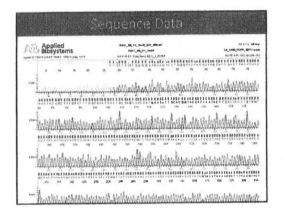

What is an Expert System for STR Data?

- A software program or set of software programs
- Performs all of these functions without human intervention
  - Identifies peaks, bands
  - Assigns alleles
  - Ensures data meet laboratory-defined criteria
  - Describes rationale behind decisions
  - No incorrect calls

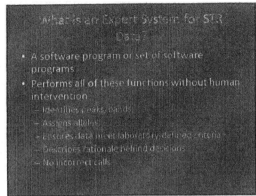

View of Peak Height Ratio Flag in GeneMapper ID

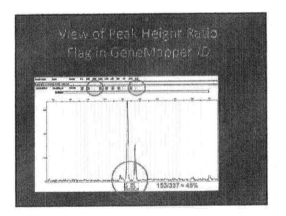

View of Preferential Amplification A:B Flag in FSS-i³

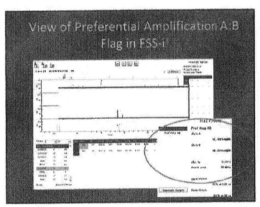

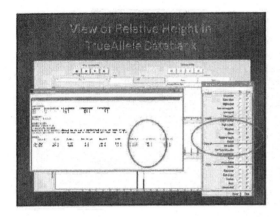

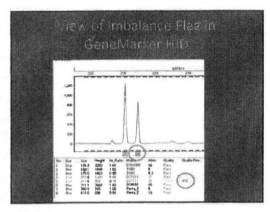

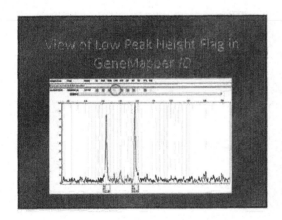

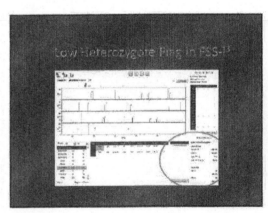

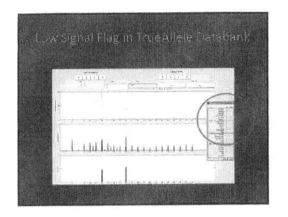

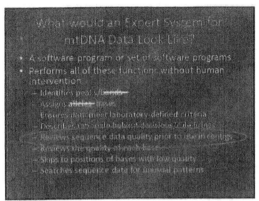

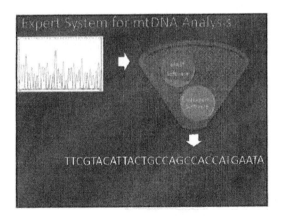

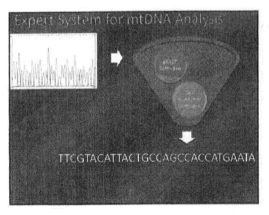

eFAST® Software

- Uses numerical information to evaluate and sort data
- Applies expert system rules to evaluate sequence data
- Sends immediate electronic message to analyst
- Does not require review of data to build contigs

Numerical Data

- Trace Score
  - Average quality value (QV) of the post-trim sequence
- Contiguous Read Length (CRL)
  - Longest, uninterrupted stretch of bases with a QV of at least 20

Sequence Scanner Software v1.0

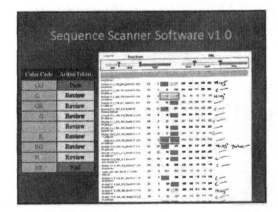

Amplification and Cycle Sequencing Strategy

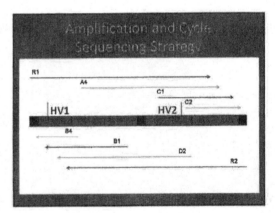

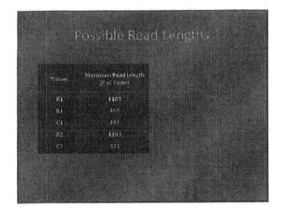

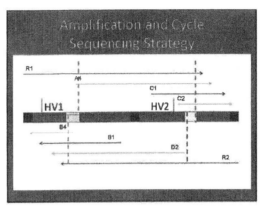

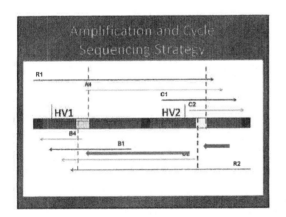

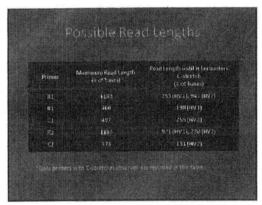

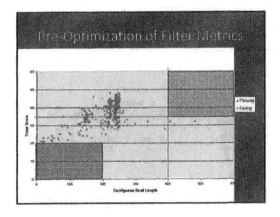

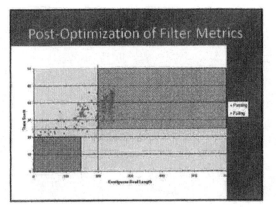

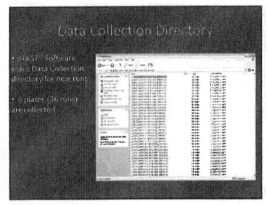

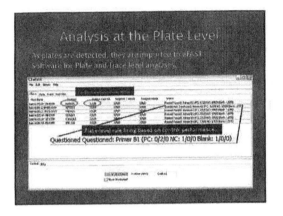

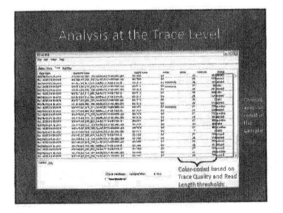

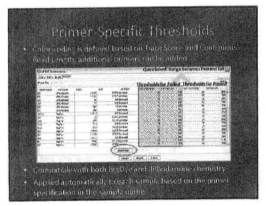

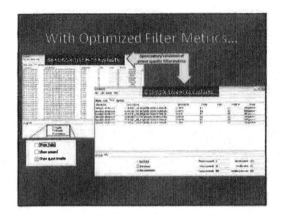

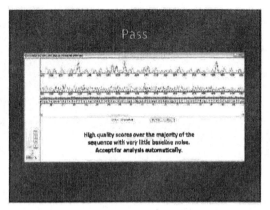

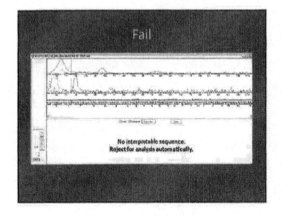

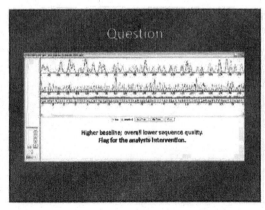

File Distribution and Sorting

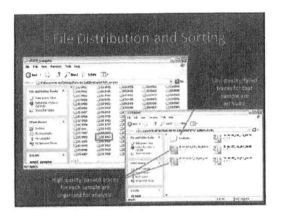

Email Notification

- At the end of the plate analysis, an email can be sent to summarize the results.

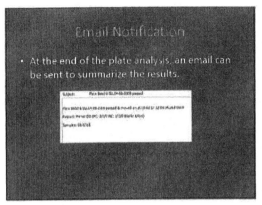

Sample Report

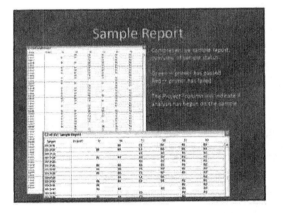

Use of Sample Directories

- Moves trace files into appropriate directories
  - Sample directory
  - Batch directory
- Automates the building of contigs
- Proceeds with data analysis using a downstream software sequence analysis program

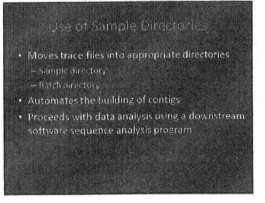

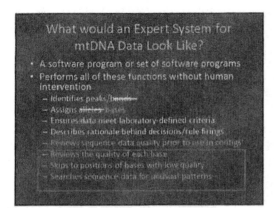

What would an Expert System for mtDNA Data Look Like?

- A software program or set of software programs
- Performs all of these functions without human intervention
  - Identifies peaks/bands
  - Assigns alleles/bases
  - Ensures data meet laboratory-defined criteria
  - Describes rationale behind decisions/rule firings
  - Reviews sequence data quality prior to use in contigs
  - Reviews the quality of each base
  - Skips to positions of bases with low quality
  - Searches sequence data for unusual patterns

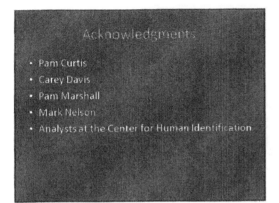

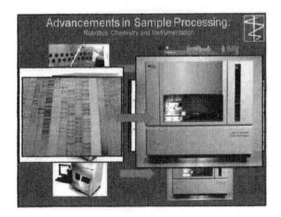

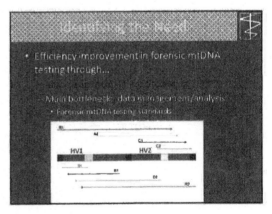

10/15/2010

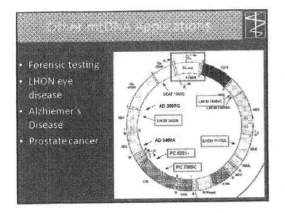

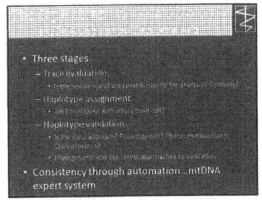

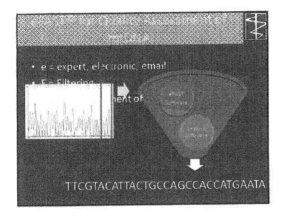

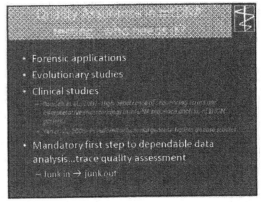

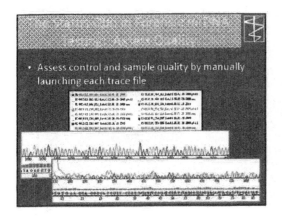

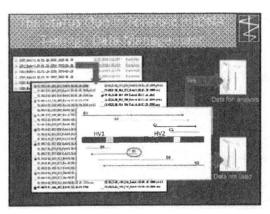

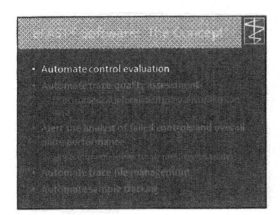

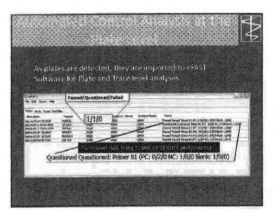

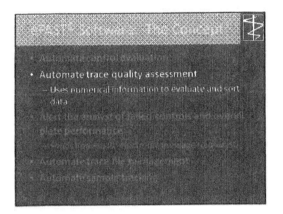

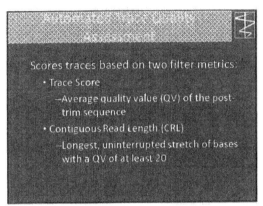

Scores traces based on two filter metrics:
- Trace Score
  - Average quality value (QV) of the post-trim sequence
- Contiguous Read Length (CRL)
  - Longest, uninterrupted stretch of bases with a QV of at least 20

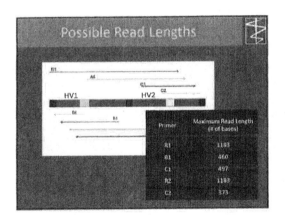

Possible Read Lengths

Primer	Maximum Read Length (# of bases)
A1	1183
B1	460
C1	497
A2	1183
C2	373

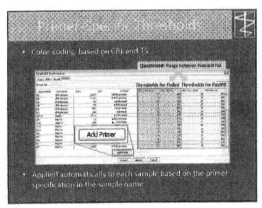

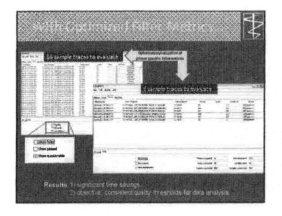

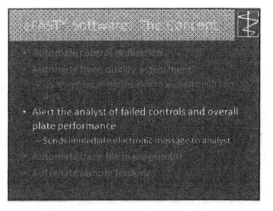

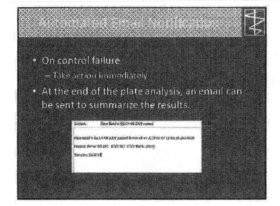

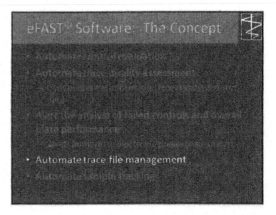

10/15/2010

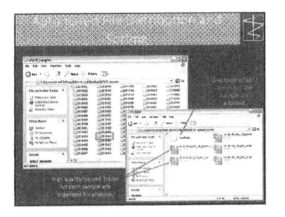

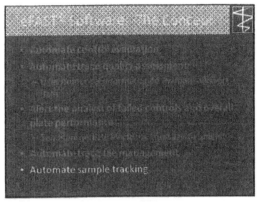

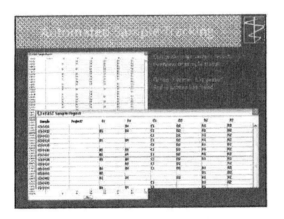

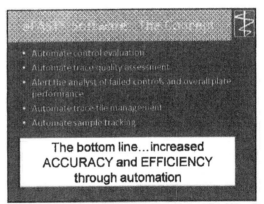

The bottom line...increased
ACCURACY and EFFICIENCY
through automation

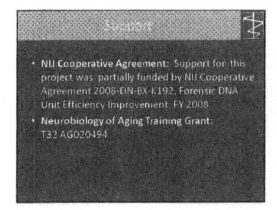

Support

- NIJ Cooperative Agreement: Support for this project was partially funded by NIJ Cooperative Agreement 2008-DN-BX-K192, Forensic DNA Unit Efficiency Improvement, FY 2008
- Neurobiology of Aging Training Grant: T32 AG020494

Acknowledgements

- Technology Transfer Group
  - Dr. Robert McClain, Elaine White
- Jennifer Thomas
- Pam Curtis
- Kisha Nutall
- Dr. Singh and the IAADR

Center for Human
IDENTIFICATION

Laboratory of Forensic Anthropology • Laboratory for Molecular Identification

Improving Efficiency in the (Mitochondrial) DNA Laboratory

NIJ Cooperative Agreement 2008-DN-BX-K192
Forensic DNA Unit Efficiency Improvement, FY 2008

Rhonda K. Roby, PhD, MPH
Department of Forensic & Investigative Genetics
Institute of Investigative Genetics

The NIJ Conference 2010
June 16, 2010
Washington, DC

Goals

- Chemistry
  - Sequencing chemistry optimization; reduced reaction volumes for commercial kits
- Robotics
  - Programmed for sequencing and commercial kit assays
- Software
  - Autofill worksheets; eFAST™ Software for sorting sequence data; enhancement of LIMS

Goals

- Chemistry
  - Sequencing chemistry optimization; reduced reaction volumes for commercial kits
- Robotics
  - Programmed for sequencing and commercial kit assays
- Software
  - Autofill worksheets; eFAST™ Software for sorting sequence data; enhancement of LIMS

---

mtDNA Processing

- Amplification of large amplicon
- Reduced reaction volume
- Reduced primer concentration
- Reduced ExoSAP-IT volume
- Reduced BigDye v1.1 chemistry
- BetterBuffer
- Xterminator/SAM solution
- eFAST™ Software

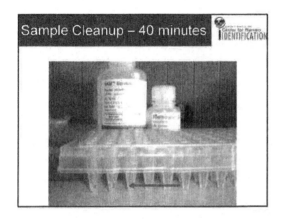

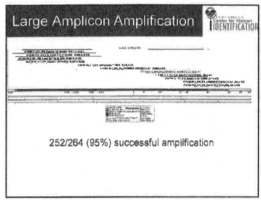

252/264 (95%) successful amplification

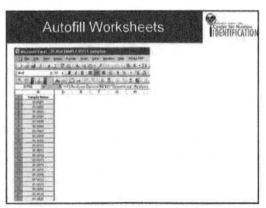

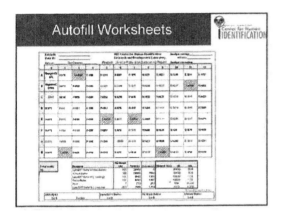

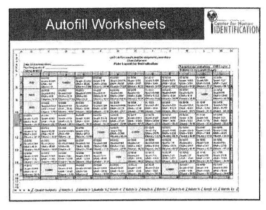

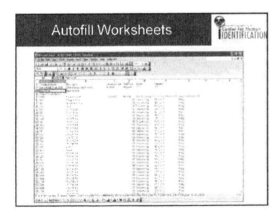

eFAST™ Software

- e = expert, electronic, email
- F = Filtering
- A = and Assessment of
- S = Sequence
- T = Traces

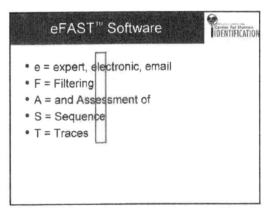

Sequence Data

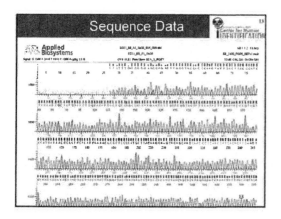

What is an Expert System for STR Data?

- A software program or set of software programs
- Performs all of these functions without human intervention
  - Identifies peaks/bands
  - Assigns alleles
  - Ensures data meet laboratory-defined criteria
  - Describes rationale behind decisions
  - No incorrect calls

View of Peak Height Ratio Flag in GeneMapper *ID*

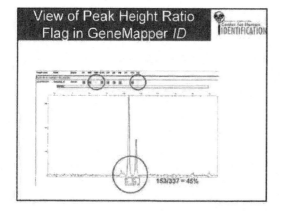

What would an Expert System for mtDNA Data Look Like?

- A software program or set of software programs
- Performs all of these functions without human intervention
  - Identifies peaks/bands
  - Assigns ~~alleles~~ bases
  - Ensures data meet laboratory-defined criteria
  - ~~Describes rationale behind decisions/rule firings~~
  - Reviews sequence data quality prior to use in contigs
  - ~~Reviews the quality of each base~~
  - Skips to positions of bases with low quality
  - Searches sequence data for unusual patterns

Expert System for mtDNA Analysis

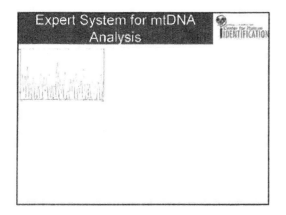

Expert System for mtDNA Analysis

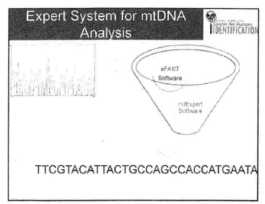

TTCGTACATTACTGCCAGCCACCATGAATA

eFAST™ Software

- Uses numerical information to evaluate and sort data
- Applies expert system rules to evaluate sequence data
- Sends immediate electronic message to analyst
- Does not require review of data to build contigs

Numerical Data

- Trace Score
  - Average quality value (QV) of the post-trim sequence
- Contiguous Read Length (CRL)
  - Longest, uninterrupted stretch of bases with a QV of at least 20

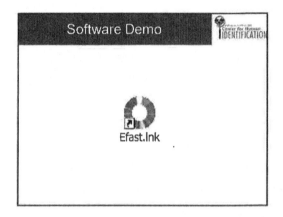

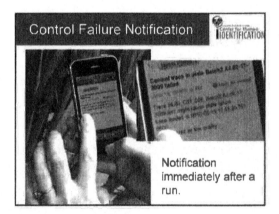

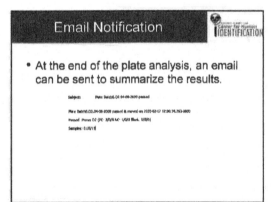

Expert System Rules and Software Advancements for Mitochondrial DNA Analysis

Nicole R. Phillips*, MS; Rhonda K. Roby, PhD MPH
University of North Texas Health Science Center
Department of Forensic and Investigative Genetics

UNT HEALTH SCIENCE CENTER

February 25, 2011

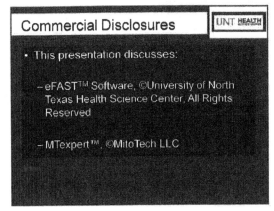

Commercial Disclosures

UNT HEALTH

- This presentation discusses:

  – eFAST™ Software, ©University of North Texas Health Science Center, All Rights Reserved

  – MTexpert™, ©MitoTech LLC

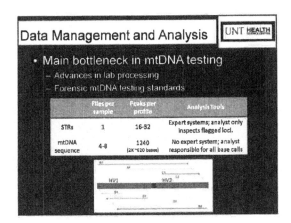

Data Management and Analysis

UNT HEALTH

- Main bottleneck in mtDNA testing
  - Advances in lab processing
  - Forensic mtDNA testing standards

	Files per sample	Peaks per profile	Analysis Tools
STRs	1	16-32	Expert systems; analyst only inspects flagged loci.
mtDNA sequence	4-8	1240 (2X ~620 bases)	No expert system; analyst responsible for all base calls

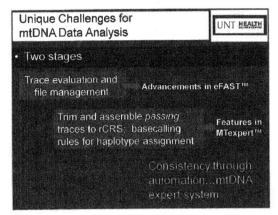

Unique Challenges for mtDNA Data Analysis

UNT HEALTH

- Two stages

  Trace evaluation and file management — Advancements in eFAST™

  Trim and assemble *passing* traces to rCRS; basecalling rules for haplotype assignment — Features in MTexpert™

  Consistency through automation…mtDNA expert system

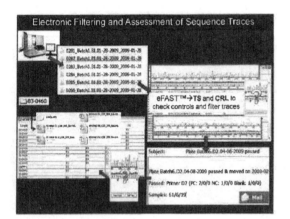

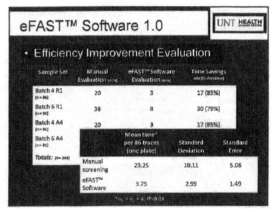

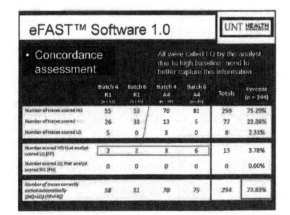

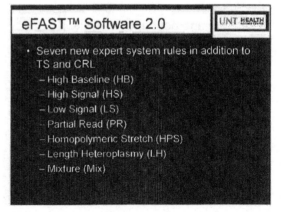

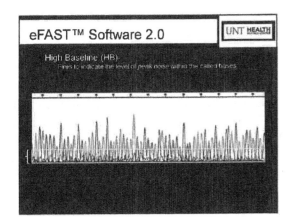

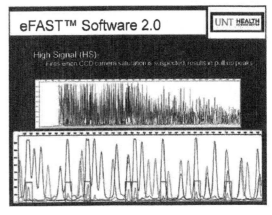

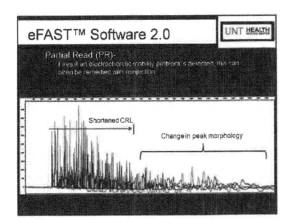

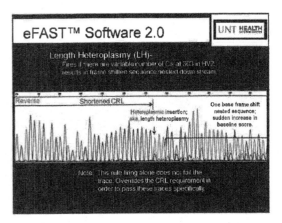

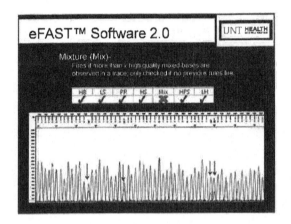

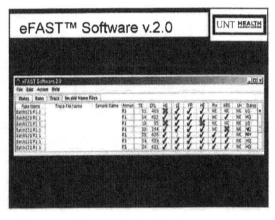

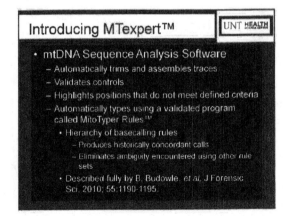

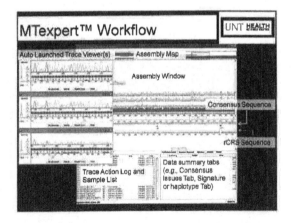

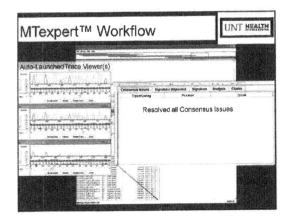

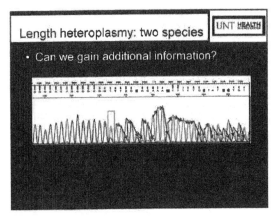

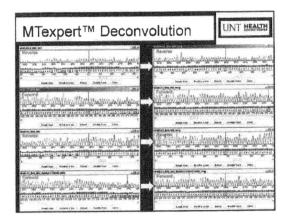

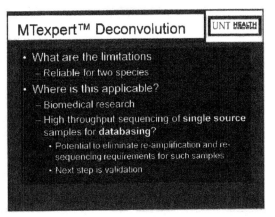

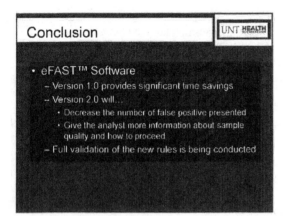

Conclusion — UNT HEALTH

- eFAST™ Software
  - Version 1.0 provides significant time savings
  - Version 2.0 will...
    - Decrease the number of false positive presented
    - Give the analyst more information about sample quality and how to proceed
  - Full validation of the new rules is being conducted

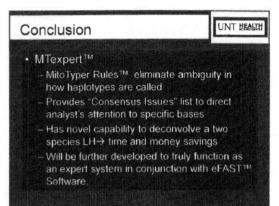

Conclusion — UNT HEALTH

- MTexpert™
  - MitoTyper Rules™ eliminate ambiguity in how haplotypes are called
  - Provides "Consensus Issues" list to direct analyst's attention to specific bases
  - Has novel capability to deconvolve a two species LH→ time and money savings
  - Will be further developed to truly function as an expert system in conjunction with eFAST™ Software.

Acknowledgements — UNT HEALTH

- The UNT Center for Human Identification
- Programmers at MitoTech LLC
- R&D Coworkers
  - Jennifer Thomas
  - Pam Curtis
  - Marc Sprouse
  - Spence Fast

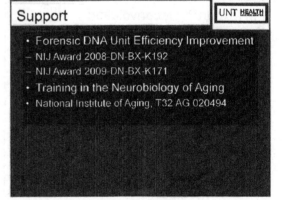

Support — UNT HEALTH

- Forensic DNA Unit Efficiency Improvement
  - NIJ Award 2008-DN-BX-K192
  - NIJ Award 2009-DN-BX-K171
- Training in the Neurobiology of Aging
- National Institute of Aging, T32 AG 020494

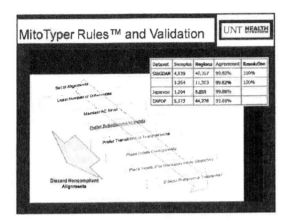

Dataset	Samples	Regions	Agreement	Resolution
SWGDAM	4,839	40,357	99.83%	100%
	1,254	11,503	99.82%	100%
Japanese	1,204	8,059	99.88%	
EMPOP	5,173	44,278	99.88%	

MitoTyper Rules™ and Validation

UNT HEALTH

UNIVERSITY OF NORTH TEXAS
Center for Human IDENTIFICATION

HIGH THROUGHPUT PROCESSING AND INCREASED EFFICIENCY FOR MITOCHONDRIAL DNA TESTING: ROBOTICS, AUTOMATED SAMPLE TRACKING, AND FILTER METRICS

Rhonda K. Roby, PhD, MPH*; Jennifer L. Thomas, MS; Nicole Phillips, BS; Suzanne D. Gonzalez, PhD;
John V. Planz, PhD; and Arthur J. Eisenberg, PhD

University of North Texas Health Science Center, Department of Forensic and Investigative Genetics,
Center for Human Identification, Fort Worth, Texas 76107

Purpose:

Robotics:

Pre-PCR MiniPrep Setup

Pre-PCR MiniPrep Setup

Post-PCR MiniPrep Setup
Cycle Sequencing Reactions

Automated Sample Tracking and Filter Metrics:

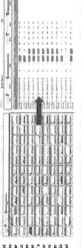

Conclusions:

The Chilean Population Database Project: A High Throughput Approach for DNA Profiling of 1000 Chilean Population Samples

Nicole R. Phillips[1], BS; Jennifer L. Thomas[1], MS; Jaime A. Pantoja[2], BS; Suzanne D. Gonzalez[1], PhD; John V. Planz[1], PhD; Arthur J. Eisenberg[1], PhD; Rhonda K Roby[1], PhD, MPH

[1] University of North Texas Health Science Center, Department of Forensic and Investigative Genetics, Fort Worth, Texas
[2] Servicio Médico Legal, Programa de Derechos Humanos, Gobierno de Justicia, Ministerio de Justicia, Santiago, Chile

Introduction

Automated Sample Tracking

Methods

Results

Figure 1.
Sample collection and the cycle

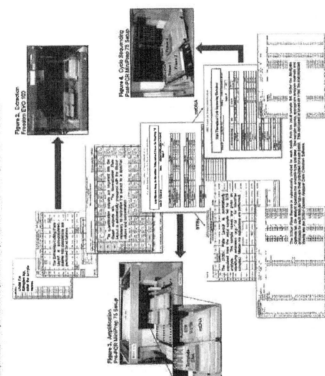

Figure 2. Extraction
Freedom EVO HD

Figure 3. Amplification
Pre-PCR MiniPrep 75 Setup

Figure 4. Cycle Sequencing
Post-PCR MiniPrep 75 Setup

Figure 5. Automated Sample Tracking and Worksheet Flow Chart

Expert Systems

Figure 6. Examples of GeneMapper ID Rule Flags

Figure 7. Filter Metrics for mtDNA Sample Screening

Conclusions

Autosomal STR Allele Frequencies and Y-STR and mtDNA Haplotypes in Chilean Sample Populations

Gonzalez, S.D.[1,2], Roby, R.K.[1,2], Phillips, N.R.[1,2], Planz, J.V.[1,2], Thomas, J.L.[1,2], Pantoja Astudillo, J.A.[3], Ge, J.[1,2], Aguirre Morales, E.[3]; Eisenberg, A.J.[1,2], Chakraborty, R.[4], Bustos, P.[3], and Budowle, B. [1,2]

[1]Department of Forensic and Investigative Genetics, University of North Texas Health Science Center, Ft Worth, Texas 76107, USA
[2]Institute of Investigative Genetics, University of North Texas Health Science Center, Ft. Worth, Texas, 76107, USA
[3]Servicio Médico Legal, Ministerio de Justicia, Gobierno de Chile, Santiago, Chile
[4]Department of Environmental Health, University of Cincinnati, Cincinnati, Ohio, 45267, USA

Introduction

A population database for the country of Chile was developed using three genotyping systems: autosomal STRs (Table 1), Y-STRs (DYS19, DYS385a/b, DYS389I, DYS389II, DYS390, DYS391, DYS392, DYS393, DYS437, DYS438, DYS439, DYS448, DYS456, DYS458, DYS635, Y-GATA-H4), and mtDNA sequences encompassing HV1 and HV2. The populations were selected to develop reference databases to support forensic casework and relationship testing.

Materials and Methods

A total of 1,020 buccal swabs were collected from male individuals in five different locations of the country from north to south: Iquique, Santiago, Concepción, Temuco, and Punta Arenas (Figure 1). The birthplaces of the individuals were noted at the time of collection in order to examine the demographic heterogeneity within the sampling sites.

DNA was extracted using the DNA IQ™ System (Promega Corporation, Madison, USA) on the Tecan Freedom EVO® 100 (Tecan Group Ltd., Männedorf, Switzerland) [1]. The STR loci were genotyped with the AmpFLSTR® Identifiler® [2] and Yfiler® PCR Amplification Kits [3] (Applied Biosystems, Foster City, USA). The mtDNA was sequenced using BigDye® Terminator v.1.1 Cycle Sequencing Kit (Applied Biosystems). All samples were subjected to electrophoresis on the ABI Prism® 3130xl Genetic Analyzer (Applied Biosystems).

Allele frequencies for 15 autosomal STR loci were calculated based on five collection localities, eight birthplace groupings, and total population. Autosomal STR data were tested for deviation from Hardy-Weinberg equilibrium (HWE) and linkage equilibrium expectations using permutation-based empirical tests. A STRUCTURE analysis was performed. F_{ST}, PD (power of discrimination), PE (power of exclusion), and related statistics were evaluated to study the utility of this database for forensic casework and relationship testing.

Results and Discussion

Individuals sampled from the five sites were not necessarily born in geo-political regions close to the sampling sites. Hence, there is an overlap in the birthplaces of subjects sampled among the sampling sites. In addition, birthplace distribution of individuals across five sampling sites was statistically different from each other. To examine possible genetic heterogeneity in the country, the pooled data were re-grouped according to their birthplaces into eight geo-political regions.

Birth Group	Region	Name	Capital
I, XV	XV	Arica y Parinacota	Arica
A	I	Tarapacá	Iquique
	II	Antofagasta	Antofagasta
B	III	Atacama	Copiapó
	IV	Coquimbo	La Serena
	V	Valparaíso	Valparaíso
C	RM (XIII)	Metropolitana de Santiago	Santiago
D	VI	O'Higgins	Rancagua
	VII	Maule	Talca
E	VIII	Biobío	Concepción
F	IX	La Araucanía	Temuco
G	XIV	Los Ríos	Valdivia
	X	Los Lagos	Puerto Montt
H	XI	Aysén del General Carlos Ibáñez del Campo	Coihaique
	XII	Magallanes y de la Antártica Chilena	Punta Arenas

Figure 1: Detailed Map of Geo-Political Regions of Chile and Sample Collection Sites. A total of 1,020 buccal swabs were collected from male individuals in five different locations (★) of the country from north to south: Iquique, Santiago, Concepción, Temuco, and Punta Arenas. Samples were re-grouped into 8 birthplace regions, as birthplaces were distributed across 15 geo-political regions regardless of sample collection site. The 8 birthplace regions are as follows: A. Regions I, II, and XV; B. Regions III, IV, and V; C. Region RM (XIII); D. Regions VI and VII; E. Region VIII; F. Region IX; G. Regions X and XIV; H. Regions XI and XII. Corresponding region names and capitals are listed above.

Results and Discussion

Autosomal STRs

In total, 986 15-locus autosomal profiles were obtained. The eight birthplace groups did not show any appreciable difference in allele frequencies at the 15 STR loci (largest F_{ST} between groups is 0.00445). No deviations from HWE and LD were detected. The number of observed deviations from linkage equilibrium was fewer than would be expected to be observed by chance within each birthplace group and the pooled dataset.

A STRUCTURE analysis, supported with the distribution of shared alleles and genotypes between all pairs of individuals, also supports the use of a pooled database for forensic applications in the country. Descriptive statistics of the autosomal STRs are provided in Table 1.

Table 1. Descriptive Statistics for Autosomal STRs for Pooled Chilean Dataset. Total number of alleles detected (No. of Alleles), range of repeat units detected in database, observed and expected heterozygosity values (H_{obs} and H_{exp} respectively), corresponding p-value for deviations from HWE, power of discrimination (PD), power of exclusion (PE), and mean power of exclusion for deficiency cases (Def) and standard trios (Trio) are reported for each corresponding locus. No deviations from HWE expectations (p < 0.05) and LD were detected. Combined PD and PE for each population exceeded 0.99999.

Y-STR Haplotypes

Y-STR haplotype data from 978 individuals yielded 803 distinct haplotypes with 688 haplotypes observed only once in the total dataset (Figure 2, Table 2). The most common Y-STR haplotype was observed seven times. Comparisons of autosomal profiles of individuals who share the same Y-STR haplotype suggest that some individuals may be biologically related. The F_{ST} based on Y-STR haplotype diversity for the total database is 0.00061 with a corresponding PD of 0.99841.

Shared Y-STR Haplotypes
2.74%, 0.87%, 0.62%, 0.12%, 0.12%, 85.69%

Figure 2. Shared Y-STR Haplotypes. Numbered legend represents the number of individuals who share a given haplotype (N=978). A total of 688 individuals (85.69%) had a unique haplotype in this dataset. The most common Y-STR haplotype was shared by seven individuals.

Shared Haplotype Count	Number of Observed Haplotypes	Haplotype Frequency
1	688	0.00102
2	79	0.00204
3	22	0.00307
4	7	0.00409
5	5	0.00511
6	1	0.00613
7	1	0.00716

Table 2. Y-STR Haplotype Frequencies. Y-STR haplotype data from 978 individuals yielded 803 observed haplotypes. Haplotype frequencies are calculated using the counting method based on the number of individuals with a shared haplotype.

Results and Discussion

mtDNA Haplotypes

Of 1007 mtDNA profiles generated, 641 distinct mtDNA haplotypes were observed (Figure 3, Table 3). The most common mtDNA haplotype was observed 16 times in the population. The F_{ST} for the mtDNA database is 0.00145 with a corresponding PD of 0.99684.

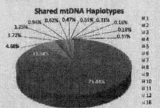

Shared mtDNA Haplotypes
0.94%, 0.62%, 0.47%, 0.31%, 0.31%, 0.16%, 1.25%, 0.16%, 1.72%, 0.31%, 4.68%, 76.44%

Figure 3. Shared mtDNA Haplotypes. Numbered legend represents the number of individuals who share a given haplotype (N=1007). A total of 490 individuals have a unique mtDNA haplotype (76.44% in this dataset). The two most common mtDNA haplotype were each shared by 16 individuals.

Shared Haplotype Count	Number of Observed Haplotypes	Haplotype Frequency
1	490	0.00099
2	81	0.00199
3	30	0.00298
4	11	0.00398
5	8	0.00497
6	6	0.00596
7	4	0.00696
8	3	0.00795
9	2	0.00895
10	2	0.00994
11	1	0.01093
12	1	0.01193
16	2	0.01590

Table 3. mtDNA Haplotype Frequencies. mtDNA haplotype data from 1007 individuals yielded 641 observed haplotypes. Haplotype frequencies are calculated using the counting method based on the number of individuals with a shared haplotype.

Conclusions

- STRUCTURE analysis supports the use of the combined dataset for forensic casework and relationship testing in Chile.
- The 8 birthplace regions do not show significant differences of allele frequencies at these 15 autosomal loci.
- The pooled dataset showed no deviation from Hardy-Weinberg Expectation of genotype frequencies for any of the 15 autosomal loci.
- Observed deviations from linkage equilibrium were smaller than that expected by chance.
- Autosomal STR loci and Y-STR and mtDNA haplotypes of these datasets are mutually independent.
- For the Y-STR and mtDNA haplotypes, the counting method can be used with appropriate correction for sampling error and with a modest level of population substructure adjustment, if necessary.
- Statistics with autosomal STR, Y-STR, and mtDNA data may be combined using the product rule.

References

[1.] F. Pepper, R. Roby, J. Planz, and A. Eisenberg. High throughput processing of family reference samples for missing persons programs. The use of robotics in extraction and amplification setup for STR and mtDNA analysis. Cond. from 17th Intl. Symp. on Human Identification – 2006. Nashville, TN.

[2.] P. Collins, L. Hennessy, C. Leibelt, R. Roby, D. Reeder, and P. Foxall. Developmental validation of a single-tube amplification of the 13 COTIS STR loci, D2S1338, D19S433 and Amelogenin. J. Forensic Sci. 49 (6) (2004) 1265-1277.

[3.] J. Mulero, C Chang, L. Calandro, R. Green, Y. Li, C. Johnson, and L. Hennessy. Development and validation of the AmpFLSTR® Yfiler™ PCR Amplification Kit: A male specific, single amplification 17 Y-STR multiplex system. J. Forensic Sci. 51 (1) (2006) 64-75.

Acknowledgements

We would like to thank Helen Costa, Elizabeth Feller, Linda LaRose, and Pamela Marshall for their contributions to the work.

PROSTATE CANCER SAMPLE REPOSITORY OF SERA AND DNA

Kisha Nutall[1]; Jennifer Thomas, MS[1]; Spence Fast[1]; Praveenkumar Shetty, PhD[2]; Jamboor Vishwanatha, PhD[2,3]; and Rhonda Roby, PhD, MPH[1,4]

[1]Department of Forensic and Investigative Genetics, [2]Graduate School of Biomedical Sciences, [3]Texas Center for Health Disparities, [4]Institute of Investigative Genetics
University of North Texas Health Science Center, Fort Worth, Texas 76107

ABSTRACT

African American men are 1.6 times more likely to be diagnosed with prostate cancer as well as more life years lost than Caucasians. At present, there is a lack of understanding of the major health disparities associated with prostate cancer. Methodist Health Systems Prostate Screening and Awareness Program, the Texas Center for Health Disparities, and the University of North Texas Health Science Center Department of Forensic and Investigative Genetics have collaborated to build Texas' largest repository of sera and DNA with a corresponding database of ethnicity, age and PSA levels. These specimens are unique due to the fact that participants are not yet diagnosed with prostate cancer. This repository will be an invaluable resource for prostate cancer research to conduct future testing of sera and DNA samples for the development of new biomarkers.

We have designed a barcoding system that offers accurate specimen identification and storage location information which ultimately translates to ease of retrieval of a specimen. Each participant contributes a sample of sera and whole blood for research purposes. The Freedom EVO® 100 (Tecan Group Ltd., Männedorf, Switzerland) robotic system is used to extract DNA from each of the blood samples. The Freedom EVO® 200 and onto CloneSaver Cards (Whatman, Piscataway, NJ) for long-term storage (Chart 1).

The use of this barcoding system, as well as additional high throughput procedures for the prostate cancer sample repository, will facilitate the implementation of these protocols into other laboratory settings.

INTRODUCTION

We aim to design a sera and DNA repository that is unique not only in content but also built to ensure every sample is easily traceable and retrievable. This repository will be the first in the world to contain sera and DNA samples as well as epigenetic information from participants that are at high risk, but have not yet been diagnosed with prostate cancer. To ensure the integrity of this repository, we have implemented a barcoding system for specimen identification and storage location to accurately track and retrieve the specimens within three mandates.

The Methodist Health Systems Prostate Screening and Awareness Program has been collecting blood samples from men over the age of 40 at health fairs and clinics in the Dallas metropolitan area since August 2000 (Figure 1). During collection of the samples, epigenetic information including the donor's age and race are documented to be used for further research in health disparities. These samples are analyzed by Methodist Dallas Medical Center (MDMC) for prostate specific antigen (PSA) levels, glucose levels, and lipid profiles. After testing is complete at the MDMC, the remaining sera and EDTA tubes of blood (Figure 2) are then sent to the University of North Texas Health Science Center (UNTHSC) where the sera are analyzed for Annexin A2. The samples are prepared for long-term storage and made available for research studies.

The repository has been designed for secure sample storage and easy retrieval via a barcoding system. This system can track individual specimens by location and quantity available. A highly detailed electronic paper trail for every sample in the repository is accessible. Samples will also be stored in multiple ways for redundancy. Serum and whole blood aliquots of every sample will be stored, bloodstains on FTA® Cards (Whatman) will be prepared, and extracted DNA will be applied on CloneSaver Cards (Whatman). FTA cards are an excellent medium for sample storage for future DNA testing (1,2). By storing every sample in a variety of preparations, we allow researchers easy access to specimens best suited to their studies including work on protein analysis from the sera samples as well as nuclear and mitochondrial DNA analysis on the whole blood and FTA® Card.

MATERIALS AND METHODS

When the samples are received by the Department of Forensic and Investigative Genetics, the tubes are scanned and a new unique barcode is assigned. The sera and blood tubes are placed into a barcoded rack in a 4°C refrigerator. When storing the samples, the rack number, the shelf location, and the specific refrigerator are also scanned. The sample barcode and specific location are immediately incorporated into an ongoing database with the epigenetic information which begins the electronic chain of custody for each sample.

Once there are sufficient samples for a full batch (i.e., 96 samples), the software alerts the user and the batch of samples are retrieved for processing. An aliquot of 1mL of whole blood is placed in a tube with a color-coded lid specifying race. This tube is placed in a barcoded box and stored in a -20°C freezer. An aliquot of whole blood is dispensed into a Sieptrep™ 96 Device (Promega Corp., Madison, WI) for extraction on the Freedom EVO® 100 using DNA IQ™ System (Promega Corp.) (3). Whole blood from each sample is spotted onto an FTA® Card (Whatman). FTA cards for each sample are archived at room temperatures in a barcoded box.

The extract plate is placed on the deck of the Freedom EVO® 200 (Figure 3), which aliquots 5µL of DNA extract to each sample location on the CloneSaver Card. This procedure is executed using the 96 position pipette head of the Freedom EVO® 200; the 96-well transfer is performed in one step (Figure 4). The CloneSaver card is barcoded, allowed to air dry, and is ready for long-term storage at room temperature.

The remaining volume of blood is transferred into a second tube and stored in a separate box at -20°C. Other long-term storage mediums are being evaluated for the remaining extracted DNA. Every sample will be stored in multiple preparations including serum and blood stored at -20°C and an FTA® Card and CloneSaver Cards stored at room temperature (Figure 5).

Figure 3.
Immediately following DNA extraction, the lysate plate and extraction plate are stored until additional processing is needed. When processing proceeds, the DNA extract plate is placed on the Freedom EVO® 200 deck. This process is automated and efficient.

Figure 4.
A total of 5µL of extracted DNA is spotted into the center of each sample location of the CloneSaver Card using the Freedom EVO® 200. Upon application, the paper turns white.

Figure 1.
Participants reviewing paperwork prior to sample collection at the Hispanic Seventh Day Adventist Church in November 2009.

Figure 2.
Sera and blood samples are received by UNTHSC.

Figure 5.
Every sample will be stored in multiple preparations including: serum and blood stored at -20°C and FTA® Card and CloneSaver Cards stored at room temperature.

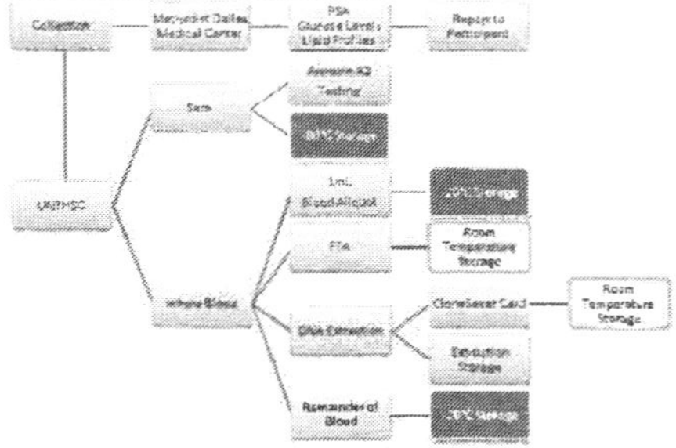

CONCLUSION

The sera and blood sample repository for prostate cancer and health disparities research housed at the University of North Texas Health Science Center is the first of its kind in the world. A repository of samples from individuals at a high-risk for developing prostate cancer will give researchers the opportunity to develop novel protein and genetic-based biomarkers for early detection of prostate cancer.

The repository uses a barcoding system to allow for highly accurate tracking and rapid retrieval of specimens even as this number of blood samples grow into the thousands. We estimate storing 14,000 samples over the next two years. Access to these samples will further protein and DNA analysis will allow us to better understand these health disparities currently seen in prostate cancer.

The protocols described in this poster can be used for barcoded storage systems for other disciplines. There is a real need to implement such high throughput procedures for accurate storage and specimen identification in order to establish an electronic chain of custody for samples used as references for forensic and human identification casework, paternity testing, and genetic databases, in general in any other biological sample repositories.

REFERENCES

1. Kline MC, Duewer DL, Redman JW, Butler JM, Bayer DA. Polymerase chain reaction amplification of DNA from aged blood stains: Quantitative evaluation of the "suitability" of four filter paper-based media. Anal Chem 2002;74:1863-1869.
2. Smith LM, Burgoyne LA. Collecting, archiving and processing DNA from wildlife samples using FTA databasing paper. BMC Ecology 2004;4:4.
3. Promega Corp (2004). Maxwell® 16 high throughput processing of forensic casework samples for multiple extraction programs. The use of robotics in extraction and analysis. Pueblo 1: 1-3.

Acknowledgments:
[funding/acknowledgment text]

Contact/Presenting Author:

Chart 1. Sample Repository Storage Flow Chart

UNIVERSITY of NORTH TEXAS
Center for Human IDENTIFICATION

Mitochondrial DNA Real-Time Quantitative PCR Assay

Marc Sprouse[1], Bruce Budowle[1,2], and Rhonda Roby[1,2]

[1]Department of Forensic and Investigative Genetics, University of North Texas Health Science Center, Fort Worth, Texas
[2]Institute of Investigative Genetics, University of North Texas Health Science Center, Fort Worth, Texas

ABSTRACT

Mitochondrial DNA (mtDNA) sequence analysis is a technique that is well characterized, validated, and a useful tool in the analysis of forensic evidence and the identification of human remains. This technique is especially useful in identifying their samples and older skeletal remains where DNA degradation is observed.

INTRODUCTION

MATERIALS AND METHODS

RESULTS

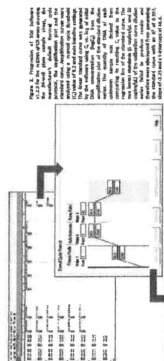

Graph 1. The quantity of DNA from both nuclear and mitochondrial DNA. For each sample (Sample 1 through Sample 10), the blue bar represents the concentration of nuclear DNA determined by use of the Quantifiler® Human DNA Quantification Kit. The red bar represents the quantity of mtDNA determined using the mtDNA qPCR assay. Of the ten samples, Samples 1 to 5 were prepared in duplicate for mtDNA; the data shown represent the mean of the two values obtained for these two samples.

Figure 2. Program of SDS Software v1.2.3 for the mtDNA qPCR assay.

SUMMARY

REFERENCES

1. Andréasson, H., et al., Real-time DNA quantification of nuclear and mitochondrial DNA in forensic analysis. BioTechniques, 2002. 33(2): 402-411.

ACKNOWLEDGEMENTS

The funding for this project was provided by the NIJ Cooperative Agreement 2008-DN-BX-K282, Forensic DNA Unit Laboratory Improvement Unit, NIJ 2008.

Assay	Multiplex w/ nuDNA	mtDNA Region	Amplicon Size (bp)
Andréasson[1] (2002)	Yes	Coding	143
Alonso[4] (2004)	Yes	Control	113/287
Walker[6] (2005)	Yes	Coding	79
Timken[7] (2005)	Yes	Coding	69
Niederstätter[8] (2007)	Yes	Coding	102/126(AS)/287(HM)

Table 1. Published multiplex qPCR assays for the simultaneous quantification of nuclear and mtDNA.

Figure 1. 7500 Real-Time PCR System with MicroAmp® Optical 96-well Reaction Plate (Applied Biosystems).

PROSTATE CANCER SAMPLE REPOSITORY OF SERA AND DNA

Kisha Nutall[1]; Jennifer Thomas, MS[1]; Spence Fast[1]; Praveenkumar Shetty, PhD[2]; Jamboor Vishwanatha, PhD[2,3]; and Rhonda Roby, PhD, MPH[1,4]

[1]Department of Forensic and Investigative Genetics, [2]Graduate School of Biomedical Sciences, [3]Texas Center for Health Disparities, [4]Institute of Investigative Genetics
University of North Texas Health Science Center, Fort Worth, Texas 76107

ABSTRACT

African American men are 1.6 times more likely to be diagnosed with prostate cancer as well as more life years lost than Caucasians. At present, there is a lack of understanding of the major health disparities associated with prostate cancer. Methodist Health Systems Prostate Screening and Awareness Program, the Texas Center for Health Disparities, and the University of North Texas Health Science Center Department of Forensic and Investigative Genetics have collaborated to build Texas' largest repository of sera and DNA with a corresponding database. These samples are unique and are a valuable resource due to the fact that participants and the diseases associated with prostate cancer. This repository will be an invaluable resource for prostate cancer research to conduct future testing of sera and DNA samples for the development of new biomarkers.

We have designed a system that offers accurate specimen identification and storage location information which ultimately translates to ease of retrieval of a specimen. Each participant contributes a sample of sera and whole blood for research purposes. The Freedom EVO® 100 (Tecan Group Ltd., Männedorf, Switzerland) robotic system is used to extract DNA from each of the blood samples. The Freedom EVO® 200 (Tecan Group Ltd.) will distribute the extracted DNA into 96-well plates and onto CloneSaver Cards (Whatman, Piscataway NJ.) for long-term storage (Chart 1).

The use of this barcoding system, as well as additional high throughput procedures for the prostate cancer sample repository, will facilitate the implementation of these protocols into other laboratory settings.

INTRODUCTION

We aim to design a sera and DNA repository that is unique not only in content but also built to ensure every sample is easily traceable and retrievable. This repository will be the first in the world to contain sera and DNA samples as well as epigenetic information from participants that are at high risk, but have not yet been diagnosed with prostate cancer. To ensure the integrity of the repository, we have implemented a barcoding system for specimen identification and storage location to accurately track and retrieve the specimens within three minutes.

The Methodist Health Systems Prostate Screening and Awareness Program has been collecting blood samples from men over the age of 40 at health fairs and clinics in the Dallas metropolitan area since August 2000 (Figure 1). During collection of the samples, epigenetic information including the donor's age and race are documented to be used for further research in health disparities. These samples are analyzed by Methodist Dallas Medical Center (MDMC) for prostate specific antigen (PSA) levels, glucose levels, and lipid profiles. After testing is complete at the MDMC, the remaining sera and EDTA tubers of blood (Figure 2) are then sent to the University of North Texas Health Science Center (UNTHSC) where the sera are analyzed for Annexin A2. The samples are prepared for long-term storage and made available for research studies.

The repository has been designed for secure sample storage and easy retrieval via a barcoding system. This system can track individual specimens for location and quantity available. A highly detailed electronic paper trail for every sample in the repository is accessible. Samples will also be stored in multiple ways for redundancy as well as for use in various research methodologies. Serum and whole blood aliquots of every sample will be stored in 96-well plates. A portion of the plasma will be spun and extracted DNA will be spotted on CloneSaver Cards (Whatman). FTA cards are an excellent medium for sample storage for future DNA testing (1,2). By storing every sample in a variety of preparations, we allow researchers easy access to specimens best suited to their studies including work on protein analysis from the sera samples as well as nuclear and mitochondrial DNA analysis on the whole blood and FTA® Card.

MATERIALS AND METHODS

When the samples are received by the Department of Forensic and Investigative Genetics, the tubes are scanned and a new unique barcode is assigned. The sera and blood tubes are placed into a barcoded rack in a 4°C refrigerator. When storing the samples, the shelf location, and the specific refrigerator are also scanned. The sample barcode and specific location are immediately incorporated into an ongoing database with the epigenetic information which begins the electronic chain of custody for each sample.

Once there are sufficient samples for a full batch (i.e. 96 samples), the software alerts the user and the batch of samples are retrieved for processing. An aliquot of 1mL of whole blood is placed in a tube with a color-coded lid specifying race. This tube is placed in a barcoded box and stored in a -20°C freezer. An aliquot of whole blood is dispensed into a Slegrec™ 96 Device (Promega Corp., Madison, WI) for extraction on the Freedom EVO® 100 using DNA IQ™ System (Promega Corp.) (3). Whole blood from each sample is spotted onto an FTA® Card (Whatman). FTA cards for each sample are archived at room temperature in a barcoded box.

The extract plate is placed on the deck of the Freedom EVO® 200 which aliquots 5µL of DNA extract to each sample location on the CloneSaver Card. This procedure is executed using the 96 position pipette head of the Freedom EVO® 200; the 96-well transfer is performed in one step (Figure 4). The CloneSaver card is barcoded, allowed to air dry, and is ready for long-term storage at room temperature.

The remaining volume of blood is transferred into a second tube and stored in a separate box at -20°C. Other storage mediums are being evaluated for the remaining extracted DNA. Every sample will be stored in multiple preparations including serum and blood stored at -20°C and an FTA® Card and CloneSaver Cards stored at room temperature (Figure 5).

Chart 1. Sample Repository Storage Flow Chart

 (flow chart)

Figure 1.
Participants reviewing paperwork prior to sample collection at the Hispanic Seventh Day Adventist Church in November 2009

Figure 2.
Sera and blood samples are received by UNTHSC.

Figure 3.
Immediately following DNA extraction, the lysate plate and extraction plate are stored until additional processing is needed. When processing proceeds, the DNA extract plate is placed on the Freedom EVO® 200 deck. This process is automated and efficient.

Figure 4.
A total of 5µL of extracted DNA is spotted into the center of each sample location of the CloneSaver Card using the Freedom EVO® 200. Upon application, the paper turns white.

Figure 5.
Every sample will be stored in multiple preparations including: serum and blood stored at -20°C and FTA® Card and CloneSaver Cards stored at room temperature.

CONCLUSION

The sera and blood sample repository for prostate cancer and health disparities research housed at the University of North Texas Health Science Center is the largest of its kind in the world. Participants from the repository contribute a high-risk population that will give researchers the opportunity to develop novel protein and genetic-based biomarkers for early detection of prostate cancer.

The repository uses a barcoding system to allow for highly accurate tracking and rapid retrieval of specimens even as the number of samples grow into the thousands. We estimate storing 14,000 collection blood samples over the next two years. Access to these samples for further protein and DNA analysis will allow us to better understand the health disparities currently seen in prostate cancer.

The protocols described in this poster can be used for barcoding and storage systems for other disciplines. There is a real need to implement such high throughput procedures for accurate storage and sample identification in order to establish an electronic chain of custody. The samples used as references for forensic and human identification casework, paternity testing, and genetic databases, in general, and other biological sample repositories.

REFERENCES

1   Kline MC, Duewer DL, Redman JW, Butler JM. Polymerase chain reaction amplification of DNA from aged blood stains. Quantitative evaluation of the "suitable" for use. Anal Chem 2002;74:1863-1869.

2   Smith LM, Burgoyne LA. Collecting, archiving and processing DNA from wildlife samples using FTA databasing paper. BMC Ecology 2004;4:4.

3   Promega. Corp., Maddison, WI. Technical Manual.

Acknowledgements:

Increasing Efficiency for Mitochondrial DNA Amplification of Reference Samples By Eliminating Time-Consuming and Costly Steps

Jennifer L. Thomas, MS[1]; Nicole R. Phillips, MS[1]; Arthur J. Eisenberg, PhD[1,2]; Rhonda K. Roby, PhD, MPH[1,2]

[1]University of North Texas Health Science Center, Department of Forensic and Investigative Genetics, Fort Worth, TX
[2]University of North Texas Health Science Center, Institute of Investigative Genetics, Fort Worth, TX

Introduction

The University of North Texas Health Science Center (UNTHSC) houses a Missing Persons Program, which processes unidentified human remains and family reference samples from biological relatives for both nuclear DNA and mitochondrial DNA (mtDNA). Mitochondrial DNA sequencing is a laborious process. In forensic mtDNA testing samples are amplified and two regions of the displacement loop (D-loop) are amplified: hypervariable region 1 (HV1) and hypervariable region 2 (HV2). This process includes the following steps: DNA quantification and normalization, HV1 and HV2 amplification, cycle sequencing, electrophoresis and analysis.

The pre-amplification stages are time-consuming and expensive, decreasing the time, reagents, and steps required for DNA lysis and amplification increases efficiency and simplifies sample processing. In order to decrease the time of extraction and amplification preparation, a method for direct lysis and amplification, which obviates the need for time-consuming extraction and time-consuming reagent preparation for amplification was developed. Several components are required for mtDNA amplification: polymerase, bovine serum albumin, magnesium chloride, 10X GeneAmp® 10X PCR Buffer II (Applied Biosystems, Foster City, CA), deoxynucleotides, primers, and water. Reducing the number of reagents the analyst is required to add to the amplification reaction decreases human error and the time of master mix preparation. This approach is ideal for streamlining the processing of mtDNA testing for high quality mtDNA and is ideal for robotic implementation.

Materials and Methods

Buccal samples were collected using the Buccal DNA Collector™ (Bode Technology Group, Lorton, VA). In addition, buccal swabs were collected and analyzed on the Buccal DNA Collector™ from five individuals. Other individuals' samples commonly submitted for casework were collected from two individuals; these samples included bloodstains on different mediums, buccal swabs, and hairs. Blood was spotted on a Human ID Bloodstain Card (GE Healthcare Bio-Sciences, Piscataway, NJ) and an FTA® GeneCard (Life Technologies, Carlsbad, CA). Two buccal swabs were taken from each individual using a Solon™ Sterile polyester tipped applicator (Solon Manufacturing Co., Rhinelander, WI) and a hair with the root still intact were also taken from each individual.

In order to achieve sufficient lysis, various incubation buffers were tested. Seven commercially available buffers and eighteen in-house buffers were evaluated. A UNTHSC Incubation Buffer was determined to produce the optimal results. A small amount of UNTHSC buffer was added to each 0.2mL strip tube, or well of a 96-well plate.

A 1.2mm Harris MicroPunch (Ted Pella, Inc. Redding, CA) was used to obtain the samples. Based on previous studies, the punches from the Buccal DNA Collector were taken from distal end (1). Punches were also taken from the Human ID Bloodstain Cards, FTA GeneCards, and the buccal swabs (Figure 1); the hair root and was collected for each hair sample. To avoid carryover contamination from using the same Harris punch for mtDNA testing, a clean Buccal DNA Collector was punched in between each sample; the next sample was punched and then placed in the tube or well, and incubated in the UNTHSC Incubation Buffer for 40 minutes at 70°C. After this lysis and

Incubation step, the UNTHSC mtDNA Amplification Master Mix containing all necessary reagents required for mtDNA amplification was added directly to the lysed samples.

Following amplification, the product was purified using ExoSAP-IT® (USB Corporation, Cleveland, OH), cycle sequenced with BigDye® Terminator v1.1 (Applied Biosystems) and purified with BigDye® XTerminator™ (Applied Biosystems) and subjected to capillary electrophoresis (2).

Figure 1. Technique used to obtain a 1.2mm punch from a buccal swab. The punch is taken from the distal end of the swab in order to avoid the critical area through the middle of the swab.

Results

Blood and Buccal Samples on Buccal DNA Collector™

Following the standard amplification protocol, product obtained from five blood samples and five buccal samples were analyzed on an agarose gel (Figure 2). Each of the 10 samples produced a band on the gel, signifying amplified product was generated. The ten samples were then sequenced. Sequence traces were evaluated using Sequence Scanner Software v1.0 (Applied Biosystems). A plate overview of these results is displayed in Figure 3. Using previously determined quality scores, the quality of data is color-coded (3).

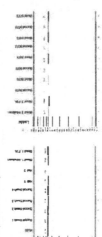

Other Common Reference Samples

Amplified product was obtained from the bloodstains on Human ID Bloodstain Cards, the bloodstains on FTA GeneCards, the buccal swabs and the hairs. These samples were analyzed on the Agilent 2100 Bioanalyzer (Agilent Technologies Inc, Santa Clara, CA) using the Agilent DNA 7500 kit (Figure 4). These samples were then sequenced. Sequence quality from these samples is displayed in Figure 6.

Figure 2. Gel image obtained from blood and buccal samples following direct mtDNA amplification of five large samples.

Figure 3. Thumbnail images explaining the raw data of the cross flow viewed in Sequence Scanner Software. Green thumbnails (at top) represent high quality sequence data, yellow thumbnails (provide overall represent medium quality data, and the red thumbnails (negative control) approach low quality/failing data.

Figure 4. Gel image of amplified product generated from other reference sample types.

Figure 5. Thumbnail images of the raw data from the hair samples, blood sample or different mediums, buccal swabs at different volumes.

Figure 6. Sequence data generated following the direct mtDNA lysis and amplification procedures showing quality sequence with little-to-no baseline noise.

Discussion

The process eliminates the need for lengthy and costly DNA extraction procedures, as well as quantification and normalization. Also, a cocktail master mix, i.e., all components in one master mix, assures considerable time-savings and reduction in overall human error. The proposed work greatly enhances the high throughput capability of mtDNA testing for high quality reference samples. This process was performed on various reference samples types and generated quality sequence data.

Reducing the number of preparation steps and sample transfers allows for the streamlining of the process and creates a procedure highly amenable to robotic adaptation. A Tecan Freedom EVO® 100 robot was incorporated to perform the automated extraction and amplification. Samples can easily be incorporated on these robotic workstations requiring minimal human intervention. This high throughput assay can easily be incorporated on these robotic workstations. Additionally, combined with automated sample punchers and liquid handling robots, this process would have minimal human intervention.

Currently, for casework application, reference samples are extracted using the DNA IQ™ System (Promega Corp., Madison, WI) on the Tecan Freedom EVO® 100 (Tecan Group Ltd, Männedorf, Switzerland) (4) and amplified for both HV1 and HV2 regions of the mitochondrial genome in separate reactions. This procedure presented here replaces the need for ready extraction simple lysis procedure and replaces two separate amplification with a single D-loop amplification (Table 1).

	UNTHSC	Proposed
Extraction	$2.10	$0.10
mtDNA Amplification	$2.98	$1.2e
Total (Per Sample)	$5.08	$1.30
Total (Per Batch of 96 Samples)	$458.88	$111.90

Table 1. Comparison of costs summarized by UNTHSC and the proposed procedure.

In addition to cost savings, considerable time-savings are achieved. The UNTHSC procedure for extracting reference samples using DNA IQ System on the Tecan Freedom EVO100System takes approximately 5 hours compared to the proposed method, which takes 40 minutes.

Conclusion

This protocol eliminates numerous time-consuming and costly steps. This procedure was performed on various samples types and produced quality sequence data. Decreasing the time to process reference samples requires to efficiently and effectively and extract and amplify a sample, greatly enhances the high throughput capability of mtDNA testing.

The cost savings associated with this method are significant. If this method was used by UNTHSC, the savings per batch are approximately $326.98. Effectively decreasing the time, human error, and cost for processing a sample leads to greater efficiency for the laboratory.

References

1. DeJte, S., Curtis, P., Sinclair, T., Weires, J., Turrough, M., Roby, R., Eisenberg, A. Optimization and the New DNA Collector. Poster Presentation. University of North Texas Health Science Center Appreciation Day. DNA Gathering. Poster Presentation. University of North Texas Health Science Center Appreciation Day -2010 Fort Worth, TX

2. Roby, R., Wilkerson, D., Jossarand, P., Parra, J., Lindille, J., Eisenberg, A. Streamlining Mitochondrial DNA Sequencing of Reference Samples. Poster Presentation. Eighteenth International Symposium on Human Identification. October, 2007, Hollywood, CA

3. Curtis, P. Thomas, J., Phillips, N., Roby, R. Optimization of Primer Specific Size Metrics for the Assessment of Mitochondrial DNA Sequence Data Mitochondrial DNA. In Press

4. Phipps, E. R. Roby, J. Parra, and A. Eisenberg. 2006. High throughput automated of family reference samples for nuclear genetic analysis. These are phases in optimization robotic setup for STR and mtDNA analysis. Genetic Identity Conference Proc. 17th International Symposium on Human Identification. October, 2006, Nashville, Tennessee

Acknowledgements
This work was funded by the National Institute of Justice.

Relevant Procedures

1. Human DNA Quantification using Reduced Reaction Volume Applied Biosystems Quantifiler® Human DNA Quantification Kit; Research & Development Laboratory

2. Human mtDNA Quantification using a Real-Time qPCR Assay; Research & Development Laboratory

3. Normalization Procedure for Extracted DNA; Research & Development Laboratory, Rev. 1

4. High Throughput Amplifications with the MiniPrep 75 Sample Processor; Research & Development Laboratory, Rev. 2

5. Manual mtDNA Amplification Setup, Rev. 1; Research & Development Laboratory

6. Post-PCR mtDNA Processing; Research & Development Laboratory, Rev. 1

7. mtDNA Sequence Analysis; Research & Development Laboratory

UNT Center for Human Identification
Procedure Manual – Research & Development Laboratory

Human DNA Quantification using Reduced Reaction Volume Applied Biosystems Quantifiler® Human DNA Quantification Kit

Purpose: The Quantifiler™ Human DNA Quantification Assay is designed to quantify the total amount of amplifiable human (and higher primate) DNA in a sample. The results from using the kit can aid in determining: 1) if sufficient human DNA is present to proceed with further DNA testing; and 2) how much sample to use in DNA analysis applications. Aside from being more cost effective, the ability to successfully reduce Quantifiler™ reaction volumes will further reduce the amount of DNA that is consumed prior to DNA typing.

The assay is comprised of two simultaneous amplifications. The first amplification is a human specific assay that consists of two primers and one TaqMan® MGB probe labeled with FAM dye for detecting the amplified human sequence. The second amplification is an internal PCR control (IPC) that consists of a synthetic template not found in nature, two primers, and one TaqMan® MGB probe labeled with VIC dye for detecting the amplified IPC DNA.

Preparation for Testing

When handling any potentially biohazardous material, always wear personal protective equipment and follow standard precautions. All personnel working with biological specimens must wear a lab coat, powderless gloves, and eye protection.
1. Verify identification numbers of samples as appropriate.
2. Prepare fresh quantification standards every two days.
3. Clean benchtops with 10% bleach solution.
4. Store Human Primer Mix at -15°C to -25°C.
5. Store PCR Reaction Mix at 2°C to 8°C. It arrives at -20°C. Upon first use, thaw, vortex gently, store at 2°C to 8°C for remainder of kit life.
6. Do not vortex PCR Reaction Mix except upon first thaw.
7. Do not place plate on diaper pads or any type of item that will pick up fluorescent fibers; place in 96-well base.
8. Use the Quantifiler™ worksheet with this protocol to organize samples, identify their position and sample number on the plate layout, record lot numbers and document run statistics.

Equipment and Supplies

• Pipettors and aerosol barrier pipette tips
• 1.5mL and 2mL tubes
• Vortex
• Microcentrifuge
• Plate Centrifuge

• Optical Reaction Plate (PN: N801-0560)
• Plate rack/support base
• Optical adhesive cover (PN: 4311971)
• Plate sealer
• 7500 Real Time PCR System

C:\Documents and Settings\pmarshal\Desktop\Proc Reduced Quantifiler,2008.doc
Created on 01/20/2009
Created by Pam Marshall, M.S.   Page 1 of 5   Approved: _____ 012009

UNT Center for Human Identification
Procedure Manual – Research & Development Laboratory

Reagents

- TE^{-4} Buffer (stored at room temperature)
- Quantifiler Human DNA Quantification Kit (PN 4343895) (PCR Reaction Mix stored at 2°C to 8°C, Human Primer Mix at -15°C to -25°C)
- Human DNA Standards (prepare every two days, store at 2°C to 8°C)
- 9947A (0.1ng/µL and 1.0ng/µL) (stored at 2°C to 8°C)

Procedure

A. Prepare Standard Dilution Series

- **DNA quantification standards are critical for accurate data**
- **Any mistakes or inaccuracies in making the dilutions directly affect the quality of results**
- **The care used in measuring and mixing dilutions and the quality of pipettors and tips affect accuracy**
- **The standards expire 2 days from date of dilution. Standards are diluted in TE^{-4}.**

1. Label 9 tubes STD 1 through STD 8 and a tube, NTC ("no template control").
2. Dispense the proper amount of TE^{-4} into each tube (see table below).
3. Prepare STD 1:
   a. Vortex the Quantifiler Human DNA Standard (200ng/µL) 3-5 seconds.
   b. Using a new pipette tip, add 10µL of Quantifiler Human DNA Standard (200ng/µL) to the STD 1 tube.
   c. Mix the dilution thoroughly by vortexing.

Standard	Concentration (ng/µL)	TE^{-4} Amount	DNA Amount	Dilution Factor
STD 1	50	30µL	10µL stock	4X
STD 2	16.7	20µL	10µL STD 1	3X
STD 3	5.56	20µL	10µL STD 2	3X
STD 4	1.85	20µL	10µL STD 3	3X
STD 5	0.62	20µL	10µL STD 4	3X
STD 6	0.21	20µL	10µL STD 5	3X
STD 7	0.068	20µL	10µL STD 6	3X
STD 8	0.023	20µL	10µL STD 7	3X
NTC	-	20µL	--	--

C:\Documents and Settings\pmarshal\Desktop\Proc Reduced Quantifiler,2008.doc
Created on 01/20/2009
Created by Pam Marshall, M.S.   Page 2 of 5   Approved: _____ 012009

3. Select each well individually and type in/upload sample information. Close Well Inspector.
4. Click on Instrument tab and check that parameters are:
   Stage 1: 95°C 10 min, 1 cycle
   Stage 2: 95 °C 15 sec, 60°C 1 min, 40 cycles
   Sample volume: **10μL**
   9600 emulation checked
   Data collection: Stage 2, step 2
5. Save the plate document as project, date, and initials (e.g., CH-MM-DD-YY-JT)
6. Place plate in 7500 Real Time PCR System with well A1 in upper left corner. Verify the proper holding rack, i.e., plates versus tubes.
7. Click START.

D. Analyzing the Results

1. Under the Amplification Plot tab, click "analyze" (using default) or click the green arrow in menu bar at top.
2. Check standard curve quality by clicking on Standard Curve tab. An R^2 value of ≥ 0.99 indicates a close fit between the standard curve regression line and the individual C_T data points of quantification standard reactions. A slope close to -3.3 indicates 100% amplification PCR efficiency. The Y-intercept is the expected C_T value of a sample with a quantity value of 1ng/μL. Record the R^2, Slope, and Y-intercept on the worksheet.

Example

Standard Curve Values	Expected Values	Observed Values
R^2	≥ 0.99	
Slope	-2.9 to -3.3	
Y-intercept	28.5	

3. Evaluate the points of the standard curve for outliers. If the R^2 value is not $\geq$ 0.99, remove 1-3 points on the standard curve to improve the fit. Both duplicates may only be deleted for Standard 8. All other standards must have at least one point represented within the standard curve. If removal of points (3 points maximum) does not yield an R^2 value ≥ 0.99, the assay must be repeated. The slope of the curve must also meet a minimum of -2.9 or the assay must be repeated. If a value greater than -3.3 is obtained, users should interpret sample data with added caution, especially for those samples quantifying near the high or low end of the standard curve. The Y-intercept also provides added insight for data interpretation. Quantifiler data is typically an overestimate of actual sample DNA concentrations. Each whole step above the expected Y-intercept value of 28.5 theoretically represents a 2-fold overestimate in sample concentration. For a Y-intercept of 29.5, sample data can theoretically be divided by 2. For a Y-intercept of 30, sample data can theoretically be divided by 3. The 9947A 0.1ng/μL and 1.0ng/μL results provide additional benchmarks for data interpretation and adjustment.

C:\Documents and Settings\pmarshal\Desktop\Proc Reduced Quantifiler,2008.doc
Created on 01/20/2009
Created by Pam Marshall, M.S.   Page 4 of 5   Approved: _____ 012009

UNT Center for Human Identification
Procedure Manual – Research & Development Laboratory

4. Check that the no template controls (NTC) are undetermined or have a C_T value greater than 38.5.

5. Check that all IPCs were successfully amplified (under <u>amplification plot</u> tab or <u>report</u> tab). Samples for which the IPC C_T value is undetermined or significantly greater than 28 may be due to the following: 1) presence of PCR inhibitors within the sample; 2) very high concentrations of DNA within the sample; 3) a non-optimal Quantifiler assay due to possible pipetting error, evaporation, bubbles, etc.; or 4) alteration of IPC template copy number during manufacturing.

6. Export results: FILE → EXPORT → RESULTS → Desktop → Exported Runs → File Name → SAVE (as a .csv file). Transfer data. Values are reported in ng/µL.

7. Remove plate and turn off 7500 Real Time PCR System.

References:

Applied Biosystems Package Insert for Quantifiler™ Human DNA Quantification Kit. Rev C, June 28, 2005.

Validation of Reduced-Scale Reactions for the Quantifiler™ Human DNA Quantification Kit, Christian G. Westring, et.al, JFS, September 2007, Vol. 52, No. 5 (1035-1043).

Revision History

Revised by	Revision Number	Revision Date

C:\Documents and Settings\pmarshal\Desktop\Proc Reduced Quantifiler,2008.doc
Created on 01/20/2009
Created by Pam Marshall, M.S.   Page 5 of 5   Approved: _____ 01 2009

UNT Center for Human Identification
Procedure Manual – Research & Development Laboratory

Human mtDNA Quantification using a Real-Time qPCR Assay

Purpose: This method quantifies the total amount of amplifiable human mitochondrial DNA (mtDNA) in sample preparations via real-time, quantitative PCR (qPCR). The results from using the assay can aid in determining: 1) if the sample contains sufficient human mtDNA to proceed with downstream mtDNA sequence analysis; 2) the amount of sample to use in PCR amplification of the mtDNA control region; and, 3) if PCR inhibitors are present in a sample that may require additional modification before proceeding.

The assay is comprised of two simultaneous amplifications. The first amplification targets a 105 bp region within the NADH dehydrogenase subunit 5 (MT-ND5) gene which corresponds to positions 13,288 to 13,392 of the revised Cambridge Reference Sequence (rCRS-GenBank: AC_000021 gi: 115315570). This amplification uses two HPLC purified primers and one TaqMan® MGB probe labeled with a 6FAM™ reporter dye and a non-fluorescent quencher (NFQ) for detecting the amplified human sequence. The second amplification is an exogenous internal positive control (IPC) that consists of a synthetic template not found in nature, two pre-designed primers, and one TaqMan® VIC® probe with TAMRA™ quencher for detecting the amplified IPC DNA. The method is based on absolute quantification and utilizes a DNA standard dilution series of known quantities to generate a standard curve from which the quantities of mtDNA may be determined. The standard is a synthetic 115 bp ultramer which includes a signature sequence to distinguish it from naturally occurring mtDNA sequences.

These reagents are designed and optimized for use with the Applied Biosystems 7500 Real-Time PCR System and SDS Software v1.2.3.

Equipment and Supplies

- Pipettors
- Pipette tips (aerosol barrier)
- 1.5mL and 2mL tubes
- Vortex
- Microcentrifuge
- Plate Centrifuge

- Optical Reaction Plate (PN: N801-0560)
- Plate rack/support base
- Optical adhesive cover (PN: 4311971)
- Applied Biosystems 7500 Real-Time PCR System with SDS v 1.2.3

UNT Center for Human Identification
Procedure Manual – Research & Development Laboratory

Reagents

- UV irradiated molecular biology grade DNAse free H_2O
- TE^{-4} (10mM Tris-HCl, pH 8.0 0.1mM EDTA)
- TaqMan® Universal PCR Master Mix, No AmpErase® UNG
- TaqMan® Exogenous Internal Positive Control Reagents
- 10μL aliquot of mtDNA synthetic standard (dsT8sig) secondary (2°) Stock
- 45μL aliquot of 100μM amplification primers (Qfwd8 and Qrev8)
- 12.5μL aliquot of 100μM TaqMan® MGB Probe (QRL8)

Safety

Gloves, lab coats and eye protection must be worn during this procedure.

Procedure

A. Preparation for Testing

1. Verify identification numbers of samples as appropriate.

2. Clean benchtops with 10% bleach solution.

3. Launch R:\RandD_DNA and open the folder "R&D Worksheets."

4. Open the Excel file "mtDNA Real-Time qPCR Assay Worksheet."

B. Prepare Standard Dilution Series

> **Note:** DNA quantification standards are critical for accurate data. Any mistakes or inaccuracies in making the dilutions directly affect the quality of results. The care used in measuring and mixing dilutions and the quality of pipettors and tips affect accuracy. The standard dilution series should be prepared fresh for each qPCR assay. They may be used for subsequent qPCR runs during the same day provided proper storage, *i.e.*, kept on ice between runs and equilibrated to room temperature prior to use. The dilutions should be discarded at the end of the day.

1. Label eight 1.5mL microcentrifuge tubes STD1 through STD8.

2. Aliquot the appropriate volume of TE^{-4} into tubes for STD1 through STD8 (see **Table 1**).

Table 1. Volumes for the Standard Dilution Series

Standard	Concentration (pg/µL)	TE $^{-4}$ Amount (µL)	DNA Amount	Dilution Factor
STD 1	1000	494	5.88µL 2° Stock	100X
STD 2	100	90	10µL STD 1	10X
STD 3	10	90	10µL STD 2	10X
STD 4	1	90	10µL STD 3	10X
STD 5	0.1	90	10µL STD 4	10X
STD 6	0.01	90	10µL STD 5	10X
STD 7	0.001	90	10µL STD 6	10X
STD 8	0.0001	90	10µL STD 7	10X

3. Prepare STD 1:
   a. Allow the 10µL aliquot of mtDNA synthetic standard (dsT8sig) 2° stock to equilibrate to room temp.
   b. Add 5.88µL of dsT8sig 2° stock to the STD1 tube.
   c. Cap, lightly vortex, and quick spin the tube to thoroughly mix the standard.

4. Prepare STD 2-8:
   a. Using a new pipette tip, add 10µL of the previous standard to the tube for the next standard.
   b. Cap, lightly vortex ,and quick spin the tube to thoroughly mix the standard.
   c. Repeat steps 4a and 4b for the dilutions of the standards.

C. Prepare Primers and Probe

Note: Allow primer and probe stock aliquots, 45µL and 12.5µL, respectively, to properly thaw and equilibrate to room temperature. Protect the TaqMan® MGB Probe (QRL8) from light. Prepare working solutions inside the no template hood.

1. Prepare working dilution (9µM) of forward primer (Qfwd8):
   a. Using a new pipette tip, add 455µL of MBG water to the 100µM **Qfwd8** stock.
   b. Cap, vortex, and quick spin the tube.

2. Prepare working dilution (9µM) of reverse primer (Qrev8):
   a. Using a new pipette tip, add 455µL of MBG water to the 100µM **Qrev8** stock.
   b. Cap, vortex, and quick spin the tube.

UNT Center for Human Identification
Procedure Manual – Research & Development Laboratory

3. Prepare working dilution (2.5μM) of TaqMan® MGB Probe (QRL8):
   a. Using a new pipette tip, add 487.5μL of MBG water to the 100μM QRL8 stock.
   b. Cap, vortex, and quick spin the tube.

D. Prepare PCR Amplification Master Mix

Note: Prepare the PCR amplification master mix inside a hood.

1. Calculate the volume of each component needed to prepare the PCR amplification master mix using the mtDNA Real-Time qPCR Worksheet.

   Note: The total number of wells includes the number of samples, controls and standards. Calculate the volume needed for each component with a pipetting overage factor of 1.1.

Example

Number of Samples (N) = 54
Controls   = 2
Standards   = 16
Total   = 72

 72 x 1.1 ≈ 79

	Vol/Sample		# of Wells		Total Vol (μL)
TaqMan® Universal M.M.	12.5μL	X	79	=	987.5
Forward Primer (Qfwd8)	2.5μL	X	79	=	197.5
Reverse Primer (Qrev8)	2.5μL	X	79	=	197.5
TaqMan® MGB Probe (QRL8)	2.5μL	X	79	=	197.5
IPC Primers & Probe (10x)	2.5μL	X	79	=	197.5
IPC DNA (50x)	0.5μL	X	79	=	39.5
					1817

2. Pipette the required volumes of the PCR amplification master mix components into an appropriately sized and labeled tube.

3. Thoroughly mix the PCR amplification master mix 3-5 seconds then quick spin.

E. Reaction Plate Setup

Note: While preparing the 96-well optical reaction plate, keep it in a 96-well base and do not place directly on counter. Do not place plate on diaper pads or any type of item that will pick up fluorescent fibers.

1. Dispense 23µL of the PCR master mix into each reaction well.

2. Outside of hood add 2µL of standard, sample, no-template control or HL60 to the appropriate wells.

3. Seal the reaction plate with an optical adhesive cover.

4. Centrifuge the plate on the Eppendorf Centrifuge 5804 at 750 x g (2420 rpm) for 2 minutes to remove any air bubbles.

F. Running the Assay

Note: Before running the amplification reactions make sure you have turned on the Applied Biosystems 7500 Real-Time PCR System and have created the plate document for the run.

1. To set up a plate document open the 7500 Real-Time PCR System Software (SDS v 1.2.3). Select **File ⟹ New** in the menu bar.

   - To use an established template select **mtDNA Real-Time qPCR Assay Template.sdt** in the *Template* field of the New Document Wizard dialog box. In the *Assay* field make sure **Absolute Quantitation (Standard Curve)** is selected. All other fields may remain unchanged. Click **Finish.**

   - To manually create the plate document, select **Blank Document** in the *Template* field. In the *Assay* field make sure **Absolute Quantitation (Standard Curve)** is selected. All other fields may remain unchanged. Click **Finish.**

   Note: If a new plate document is manually created a dialog box will appear after clicking **Finish.** Select **ROX** in the *Passive Reference* input field and select and add to the *Detectors in Document*, the **QRL8** and **Exogenous IPC** detectors. If this is the first time using the **QRL8** and **Exogenous IPC** detectors click **New Detector** and fill in the following parameters:

Name:QRL8	Name: Exogenous IPC
Reporter Dye: FAM	Reporter Dye: VIC
Quencher Dye: None	Quencher: TAMRA

Click **OK** after creating both detectors then select and add them to the *Detectors in Document*. When completed click **Finish.**

2. Under *Setup* tab highlight wells to be used in the assay, click magnifying glass icon in the toolbar or select **View** ⟹ **Well Inspector** in the menu bar. Select the **QRL8** and **Exogenous IPC** boxes.

3. Select each empty well individually and type sample name and appropriate information.

4. Click on *Instrument* tab and check that the *Thermal Profile* parameters are:
    Stage 1: 50°C 2 min, 1 cycle
    Stage 2: 95°C 10 min, 1 cycle
    Stage 3: 95°C 15 sec, 60°C 1 min, 40 cycles
    Sample volume: 25µL
    9600 emulation (checked)
    Data collection: Stage 3, step 2

5. Save the plate document as project, date, and initials, *e.g.*, CH-MMDDYY-JT.

6. Insert plate in 7500 Real-Time PCR System with well A1 in upper left corner.

7. Click **Start**.

G. Analysis

1. Click **Analysis** ⟹ **Analysis Settings** in the menu bar and select the following:

    - **Manual C$_T$** ⟹ Threshold: 0.2
    - **Automatic Baseline**

    When finished click **OK**.

2. Click the green arrow, *i.e.*, **Analysis**, button in the task bar.

3. Review the results under the *Results* tab. Check the standard curve quality by clicking on the *Standard Curve* tab. Record the R^2, Slope, and Y-intercept on the mtDNA Real-Time qPCR Assay worksheet.

    Note: An R^2 value of greater than or equal to 0.99 indicates a close fit between the standard curve regression line and the individual C$_T$ data points of quantification standard reactions. A slope close to -3.3 indicates 100% amplification PCR efficiency. The Y-intercept is the expected C$_T$ value of a sample with a quantity value of 1.

4. Evaluate the points of the standard curve for outliers. If the R^2 value is not ≥ 0.99, remove up to three points on the standard curve to improve the fit. Both duplicates may only be deleted for Standard 8. All other standards must have at least one point represented within the standard curve. If removal of points (3 points maximum) does not yield an R^2 value ≥ 0.99, the assay must be repeated. The same is true of the slope and Y-intercept; the slope of the curve must be -3.38 ± 0.06 and the Y-intercept must equal 23.1 ± 0.7, otherwise the assay must be repeated.

5. Under the *Report* tab, check that the no-template controls (NTC) are undetermined or have a value less than the lowest standard.

6. Check that all IPCs were successfully amplified under the *Amplification Plot* tab or *Report* tab. Samples for which the IPC C_T value is undetermined or is significantly high may be due to: 1) presence of PCR inhibitors within the sample or 2) very high concentrations of DNA within the sample.

7. Export results to the desired location (as a .csv file). The values are reported in pg/μL.

8. Remove plate and turn off 7500 Real-Time PCR System.

References

1. MF Kavlick, HS Lawrence, RT Merritt, C Fisher, A Isenberg, JM Robertson, and B Budowle (in press) Quantification of Human Mitochondrial DNA Using Synthesized DNA Standards. J Forensic Sciences.

Revisions

Date of revision	Revised by	Description of changes made

Appendix A

Conversion Table for the Concentration of the Human mtDNA Genome

Note: A DNA molecular weight calculator (www.bioinformatics.org/sms2/) was used to determine the MW of the human mtDNA genome. Final MW of the human mtDNA genome is $1.699793544 \times 10^{-5}$ pg.

Standard	Concentration (pg/µL)	Concentration (copies/µL)
STD 1	1000	5.88×10^7
STD 2	100	5.88×10^6
STD 3	10	5.88×10^5
STD 4	1	5.88×10^4
STD 5	0.1	5.88×10^3
STD 6	0.01	5.88×10^2
STD 7	0.001	5.88×10^1
STD 8	0.0001	5.88

Normalization Procedure for Extracted DNA

Purpose: Before amplifying DNA samples, prepare each sample to yield appropriate DNA concentrations for the procedure being performed. Quantification results are imported into the normalization plate layout worksheet, in which subsequent dilutions are calculated for each sample.

Preparation for Testing

1. Verify identification numbers of samples as appropriate.

2. Clean benchtops with 10% bleach solution and rinse with distilled water and 70% ethanol if necessary.

Equipment and Supplies

- Pipettors
- Pipette tips (aerosol barrier)

Reagents

- Diluent (TE^{-4} buffer recommended)

Safety

Gloves, lab coats and eye protection must be worn during this procedure.

Procedure

1. Launch "Normalization plate layout" spreadsheet located on the Y:\ drive (Y:\R&D Worksheets.xls).

2. Select the tab titled *Sample quant list*. In cell J2 (i.e., *Target [DNA]*, highlighted in blue), enter the target final concentration desired for a final volume of 50µL. Refer to Appendix A for guidance.

3. Copy and paste quantification results into the "Quant outputs" tab in the normalization plate layout worksheet. The spreadsheet will automatically calculate the necessary dilutions for each sample for a final volume of 50µL.

    Note: If no dilution is required, transfer 50µL of extract to the dilution plate.

Y:\R&D Staff\Nicole\Active SOPs (word)\Active SOPs (Word)\Plate Normalization.Rev.1.doc
Created on 01/20/2009
Revised on 02/06/2009

Page 1 of 3   Approved: _____ 02 06 09

4. See corresponding tab (e.g., Batch 2) for normalization values and print the plate layout.

5. Dispense the calculated diluent volume into each labeled tube/well in the template-free hood. An assisting scientist will call out the well position and volume of diluent to be added.

6. Vortex the quantified DNA samples, then centrifuge briefly.

7. Outside of the hood, add the appropriate volume of DNA template to respective tube/well. An assisting scientist will call out the well position and volume of extract to be added. Once extract transfers are complete for the plate, confirm the absence of liquid in the ladder and control wells.

Revisions

Date of revision	Revised by	Description of changes made
02/06/2009	Rhonda K. Roby Suzanne D. Gonzalez	Modified to allow for different normalization concentrations; a second scientist was added to support the primary scientist.

Y:\R&D Staff\Nicole\Active SOPs (word)\Active SOPs (Word)\Plate Normalization.Rev.1.doc
Created on 01/20/2009
Revised on 02/06/2009

Page 2 of 3   Approved: _____ 020609

Normalization Procedure for Extracted DNA

Appendix A

For a final concentration of 0.5ng/ μL, enter 0.5 in cell J2, *Target [DNA]*.
    1 μL from normalized plate = 0.5ng DNA

For a final concentration of 0.083ng/ μL, enter 0.083 in cell J2, *Target [DNA]*.
    6 μL from normalized plate = 0.5ng DNA

Y:\R&D Staff\Nicole\Active SOPs (word)\Active SOPs (Word)\Plate Normalization.Rev.1.doc
Created on 01/20/2009
Revised on 02/06/2009

Page 3 of 3   Approved: _____ 020609

High Throughput Amplifications with the MiniPrep 75 Sample Processor

Purpose: The MiniPrep 75 Sample Processor is programmed to setup PCR amplifications for high throughput processing of samples using reduced reaction volumes. Three different scripts can be chosen by the analyst to simultaneously perform the PCR amplification setups for autosomal STR (AmpFLSTR® Identifiler® PCR Amplification Kit), Y-STR (AmpFLSTR® Yfiler® PCR Amplification Kit), and mtDNA.

Equipment and Supplies

- MiniPrep 75 Sample Processor
- Centrifuge, vortex
- Pipettors and pipette tips (aerosol barrier)
- 96-well plates and base supports (5)
- 100mL trough
- Aluminum foil plate seals or strip caps
- 1.5mL or 2mL microcentrifuge tubes
- GeneAmp® PCR System 9700

Safety

Gloves, lab coats and eye protection must be worn during this procedure.

Reagents

- Bleach (10%)
- Ethanol (70%)
- ddH$_2$O
- AmpFLSTR® Identifiler® PCR Amplification Kit
- AmpFLSTR® Yfiler® PCR Amplification Kit
- 9948 Male DNA (0.5ng/µL)
- AmpliTaq Gold Polymerase

- HL60 Control DNA (0.25ng/µL)
- Primer R1 (3µM)
  (5'-CACCAGTCTTGTAAACCGGAGA-3')
- Primer R2 (3µM)
  (5'-CTTTGGGGTTTGGTTGGTTC-3')
- dNTPs (10mM)
- PCR Buffer II (10X)
- MgCl$_2$ (25mM)
- BSA (1.6µg/µL)

Procedure

A. Preparation

Clean the deck with 10% bleach, rinse with water, and follow with 70% ethanol, if desired. Inspect and wipe the tips of the robot with 70% ethanol. Finger-tighten the syringes at both the syringe cap and plunger screw.

Note: Do not bend tips when wiping.

B. Master Mix and Control Preparation

1. Launch the Y:\ network drive and open the folder "R&D Worksheets."

2. Open the Excel file "High Throughput MiniPrep Amplification Setup."

Y:\R&D Staff\Nicole\Active SOPs (word)\Active SOPs (Word)\MiniPrep Amplification Setup.Rev.2.doc
Created on 01/20/2009
Revised on 05/19/2009   Page 1 of 8   Approved: _____ 05/2009

3. Enter the number of samples to be setup for amplification in the specified cell. The spreadsheet will automatically populate all "Sample #" cells and calculate the volume needed for each component. The calculations for the reactions are shown below.

Total volume of reagent for use on the MiniPrep	=	Volume of specified reagent needed per sample	×	Number of samples (N)	×	*Pipetting overage factor

Master Mix for Identifiler and Yfiler
(Example, $N = 90$)

Reagent	Vol. per Sample (µL)	Total Volume (µL)
AmpFLSTR PCR Reaction Mix	5.8	678.6
AmpFLSTR Primer Set	2.9	339.3
Polymerase	0.3	35.1

Pipetting overage factor = 1.3

mtDNA Amplification
Master Mix for 1µL Template Addition
(Example, $N = 90$)

Reagent	Vol. per Sample (µL)	Total Volume (µL)
Sterile H_2O	7.7	935.6
10X PCR Buffer II	1.5	182.3
BSA	1.5	182.3
dNTP mix	1.2	145.8
$MgCl_2$	0.9	109.4
Polymerase	0.6	72.9
Primer R1	0.3	36.45
Primer R2	0.3	36.45

Pipetting overage factor = 1.35

Y:\R&D Staff\Nicole\Active SOPs (word)\Active SOPs (Word)\MiniPrep Amplification Setup.Rev.2.doc
Created on 01/20/2009
Revised on 05/19/2009   Page 2 of 8   Approved: _____ 05'2009

mtDNA Amplification
Master Mix for **6µL** Template Addition
(Example, $N = 90$)

Reagent	Vol. per Sample (µL)	Total Volume (µL)
Sterile H_2O	2.7	243
10X PCR Buffer II	1.5	182.3
BSA	1.5	182.3
dNTP mix	1.2	145.8
$MgCl_2$	0.9	109.4
Polymerase	0.6	72.9
Primer R1	0.3	36.45
Primer R2	0.3	36.45

* Pipetting overage factor = 1.3

4. Print the completed worksheet for master mix preparation.

5. Prepare the necessary master mixes for the amplifications. Add the reagents in order from greatest to least volume required.

   Note: If two mtDNA amplifications are required, two mtDNA master mixes must be prepared.

6. Remove the cold block from -20°C storage and place on the instrument deck.

7. Place the master mix tubes in the cold block on the instrument deck with the lids closed.

8. Prepare two 1.5mL tubes of 9948 positive control and one tube of HL60. With the lids closed, place the three positive controls in the designated wells of the cold block as shown in the Deck Layout diagram (Figure 1).

9. Prepare three 1.5mL tubes of ddH$_2$O. With the lids closed, place the ddH$_2$O tubes in the designated wells of the cold block as shown in the Deck Layout diagram (Figure 1).

   Note: Ensure that all plates, water and other appropriate consumables have been properly UV crosslinked per protocol.

Y:\R&D Staff\Nicole\Active SOPs (word)\Active SOPs (Word)\MiniPrep Amplification Setup.Rev.2.doc
Created on 01/20/2009
Revised on 05/19/2009   Page 3 of 8   Approved: _____ 052009

Figure 1: Deck Layout

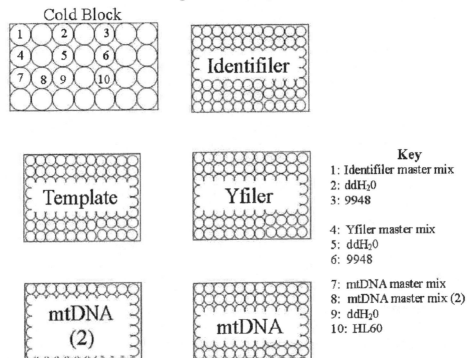

Cold Block

1	2	3
4	5	6
7	8 9	10

Identifiler

Template

Yfiler

mtDNA (2)

mtDNA

Key

1: Identifiler master mix
2: ddH$_2$0
3: 9948

4: Yfiler master mix
5: ddH$_2$0
6: 9948

7: mtDNA master mix
8: mtDNA master mix (2)
9: ddH$_2$0
10: HL60

C.   MiniPrep 75 Sample Processor Setup and Run Execution

1.   Launch Gemini software program.

2.   Choose the appropriate script:

- Open the "**Identifiler,Yfiler + mtDNA amplifications**" if adding 1µL of template DNA. This script is typically chosen when samples have been normalized to a higher concentration (0.5 ng/µL - 1.0ng/µL) using the Quantifiler® kit.

- Open the "**Identifiler,Yfiler + mtDNA amplifications 6uL**" script if adding 6µL of template DNA and performing one mtDNA amplification. This script is typically used when samples have been normalized to a lower concentration (0.083 ng/µL – 0.167ng/µL) using the Quantifiler kit.

- Open the "**Identifiler,Yfiler + TWO mtDNA amplifications 6uL**" if adding 6µL of template DNA and performing two mtDNA amplifications. Two amplifications are typically performed on population samples that have a high occurrence of HV1 homopolymeric stretches and/or HV2 length heteroplasmies.

Y:\R&D Staff\Nicole\Active SOPs (word)\Active SOPs (Word)\MiniPrep Amplification Setup.Rev.2.doc
Created on 01/20/2009
Revised on 05/19/2009   Page 4 of 8   Approved: _____ 05 2009

7. Label the necessary 96-well plates (e.g., CDB2009-01-Id). Place onto a 96-well colored bases and in the correct position on the deck (see Figure 1: Deck Layout).

   Note: Figure 1 illustrates the deck layout for double mtDNA amplification (mtDNA and mtDNA(2)). If only one mtDNA amplification is needed, leave the mtDNA(2) position empty on the deck.

8. Place the template plate in a plate base and on the MiniPrep deck (see Figure 1: Deck Layout).

9. Open the lids to the master mix and controls.

10. Select the green triangle button to start.

11. The program will prompt the operator to enter the number of columns to be processed for the left arm and the number of columns to be processed for the right arm (enter any number between 1 and 12).

    Note: The number of columns for the left arm must be the same for the right arm.

12. Once the amplification setup is complete, plates should promptly be removed and sealed. Place the plates in the thermal cyclers, and verify thermal cycling parameters with the tables provided in Section D. Initiate the run.

13. Seal the original 96-well template plate. Store plates at 4°C for short term storage and at -20°C for long term storage (longer than two weeks).

14. Return reagents and cold block to proper storage. Close the Gemini software and turn off the instrument.

15. Empty the bleach trough. Empty the waste container, if necessary. Fill system water container with NANOpure water, if necessary.

16. Clean the deck with 10% bleach, rinse with water, and follow with 70% ethanol, if desired.

Y:\R&D Staff\Nicole\Active SOPs (word)\Active SOPs (Word)\MiniPrep Amplification Setup.Rev.2.doc
Created on 01/20/2009
Revised on 05/19/2009   Page 6 of 8   Approved: _____ 052009

UNT Center for Human Identification
Procedure Manual – Research & Development Laboratory

Manual mtDNA Amplification Setup

Purpose: To manually prepare amplifications of the mitochondrial D-loop region. This amplification reaction is 15µL, producing a single amplicon which spans positions 15931-545 of the mitochondrial genome.

Equipment and Supplies

- Centrifuge, vortex
- Pipettors and pipette tips (aerosol barrier)
- 96-well plates and base supports (5)
- Aluminum foil plate seals or strip caps
- 1.5mL or 2mL microcentrifuge tubes
- GeneAmp® PCR System 9700

Safety

Gloves, lab coats and eye protection must be worn during this procedure.

Reagents

- Bleach (10%)
- Ethanol (70%)
- UV irradiated molecular biology grade DNAse free H_2O
- AmpliTaq Gold Polymerase (5U/µL)
- HL60 Control DNA (0.12pg/µL)

- Primer R1 (9µM)
  5'-CACCAGTCTTGTAAACCGGAGA-3'
- Primer R2 (9µM)
  5'-CTTTGGGGTTTGGTTGGTTC-3'
- dNTPs (10mM)
- PCR Buffer II (10X)
- $MgCl_2$ (25mM)
- BSA (1.6µg/µL)

Procedure

A. Master Mix Calculations and Preparation

1. Launch R:\RandD_DNA and open the folder "R&D Worksheets."

2. Open the Excel file "Manual mtDNA Amplification Setup."

Enter the number of samples to be setup for amplification in the specified cell. The spreadsheet will automatically populate all "Sample #" cells and calculate the volume needed for each component with a pipetting overage factor included.

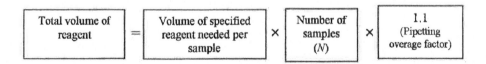

$$\text{Total volume of reagent} = \text{Volume of specified reagent needed per sample} \times \text{Number of samples } (N) \times 1.1 \text{ (Pipetting overage factor)}$$

mtDNA Amplification

Master Mix for 6μL Template Addition
(Example, $N = 10$)

Reagent	Vol. per Sample (μL)	Total Volume (μL)
Sterile H_2O	3.3	36.3
10X PCR Buffer II	1.5	16.5
BSA	1.5	16.5
$MgCl_2$	0.9	9.9
dNTP mix	0.6	6.6
Polymerase	0.6	6.6
Primer R1	0.3	3.3
Primer R2	0.3	3.3

3. Print the completed worksheet for master mix preparation; enter the appropriate lot numbers and expiration dates.

4. In the no template hood, prepare the necessary master mixes for the amplifications. Add the reagents in order from greatest to least volume required. Dispense 9μL of master mix into each well or tube, including the wells designated for positive, negative and reagent blank controls.

5. In an area designated for template addition, add 6μL of ddH_2O to the negative control well, add 6μL template to each of the sample wells and the reagent blank, add 2μL of HL60 and 4μL of ddH_2O to the positive control well(s).

   Note: A lesser quantity of HL60 may be used for amplification of regions smaller than R1/R2.

   Note: Allow the DNA template to equilibrate to room temperature; briefly vortex and quick spin the samples and HL60 prior to addition.

6. Seal the tubes/plate and briefly centrifuge.

7. Place the tubes in the retainer on the thermal cycler or the plate directly on the thermal cycler; record the thermal cycler number on the worksheet.

B. Thermal Cycling Parameters

1. Select the appropriate program.

2. Enter 15μL for the reaction volume.

3. Select START.

4. After the run is complete, samples can be electrophoresed or stored 14 days at 4°C.

Post-PCR mtDNA Processing

Purpose: Post-PCR mtDNA processing consists of post-PCR purification, cycle sequencing, and post-cycle sequencing purification. Procedures are used in conjunction with the "High Throughput Cycle Sequencing Worksheet." *Post-PCR purification*: ExoSAP-IT® treats PCR products ranging in size from less than 100 bp to over 20 kb with no sample loss by removing unused primers and nucleotides that may interfere with sequencing reactions. *Cycle sequencing:* Sequencing reactions are performed using the BigDye® Terminator v1.1 Cycle Sequencing Kit. *Post-cycle sequencing purification*: The BigDye® XTerminator™ Purification Kit is designed to sequester cycle sequencing reaction components such as salt ions, unincorporated dye terminators, and dNTPs to prevent their co-injection with dye-labeled extension products.

Preparation for Testing

1. Verify plate identification.

2. Clean benchtops and hood with 10% bleach solution and rinse with distilled water and 70% ethanol, if necessary.

3. Use hood with dedicated pipettors for handling reagents and master mix setup.

4. DNA template must remain outside the setup hood.

5. Only one reagent tube should be open at any time.

Equipment and Supplies

- Pipettors
- Pipette tips (barrier tips)
- 1.5mL microcentrifuge tubes
- Eppendorf Centrifuge 5804
- MicroAmp® Caps (Applied Biosystems, P/N 801-0534)
- Plate centrifuge
- Fisher Vortex Genie 2 with foam 96-well plate holder
- 96-well plates
- GeneAmp® PCR System 9700

Safety

Gloves, lab coats, and eye protection must be worn during this procedure.

Y:\R&D Staff\Nicole\Active SOPs (word)\Active SOPs (Word)\Post PCR mtDNA Processing.Rev 1.doc
Created on 01/24/2009
Revised on 05/20/2009   Page 1 of 6   Approved: _____ 05 2009

A. Post-PCR mtDNA Purification by ExoSAP-IT®

Reagents

- ExoSAP-IT® (stored at -20°C)

Procedure

1. Launch the Y:\ network drive and open the folder titled "R&D Worksheets."

2. Open the Excel file titled "High Throughput Cycle Sequencing Worksheet."

3. Enter the batch ID and the number of samples to be setup for post-PCR processing in the highlighted cell. For every column of samples processed, add one additional sample for pipetting overage. The spreadsheet will automatically populate all "Sample #" cells and calculate the volume needed for each component. The calculations for the reactions are shown below.

Figure 1: Reagent Calculation.

Total volume of reagent	=	Volume of specified reagent needed per sample	×	Number of samples + pipetting overage

4. Print the completed worksheet to document the lot number and expiration date of ExoSAP-IT. Complete the required fields.

5. Remove ExoSAP-IT from -20°C freezer and keep on ice/cold block during procedure.

6. Add 2µL of ExoSAP-IT to each PCR reaction tube/well containing 15µL of amplified product, yielding a total volume of 17µL per tube.

7. Note the date, thermal cycler number, lot number and expiration date of the ExoSAP-IT on worksheet. Incubate PCR tubes/plate in thermal cycler as follows:

Table 1: ExoSAP-IT Thermal Cycler Parameters

# of Cycles	Temperature	Time (min:sec)
No cycling required	37°C	15:00
	80°C	15:00
	4°C	∞

8. The PCR product is ready for use for DNA sequencing applications. Store at 2-8°C in the **Post-PCR Laboratory**.

Note: PCR product should be stored at -20°C if it is to be stored for longer than 2 weeks.

Y:\R&D Staff\Nicole\Active SOPs (word)\Active SOPs (Word)\Post PCR mtDNA Processing Rev 1.doc
Created on 01/24/2009
Revised on 05/20/2009   Page 2 of 6   Approved: _____ 05 2009

B. Cycle Sequencing Reaction Setup

Reagents

- BigDye® Terminator™ v1.1 Cycle Sequencing Kit
- BetterBuffer
- ddH$_2$O
- Sequencing primers

-A1 (5'-CACCATTAGCACCCAAAGCT-3')
-A2 (5'-TACTTGACCACCTGTAGTAC-3')
- B1 (5'-GAGGATGGTGGTCAAGGGAC-3')
-B2 (5'-GGCTTTGGGAGTTGCAGTTGAT-3')
-C1 (5'-CTCACGGGAGCTCTCCATGC-3')
-C2 (5'-TTATTTATCGCACCTACGTTCAAT-3')

- D1 (5'-CTGTTAAAAGTGCATACCGCCA-3')
- D2 (5'-GGGGTTTGGTGGAAATTTTTTG-3')
- A4 (5'-CCCCATGCTTACAAGCAAGT-3')
- B4 (5'-TTTGATGTGGATTGGGTTT-3')
- R1 (5'-CACCAGTCTTGTAAACCGGAGA-3')
- R2 (5'-CTTTGGGGTTTGGTTGGTTC-3')

Procedure

Note: The following component volumes are calculated for cycle sequencing 1μL of PCR product. The volume of PCR product can be changed (0.5μL - 7.5μL) to optimize the sequencing reaction. Adjust the volume of water added to the master mix and the volume of master mix dispensed accordingly.

1. Refer to "High Throughput Cycle Sequencing Worksheet" for the given batch number. Record reagent lot numbers and expiration dates on the worksheet.

2. Pulse vortex the BigDye Terminator v1.1, primers and BetterBuffer. Centrifuge the tubes briefly to remove any liquid from the caps.

3. The spreadsheet has automatically calculated the volume needed for each component based on the calculations in Figure 1. Totals represent necessary volumes needed for each sequencing primer.

Table 2: Master Mix for mtDNA Cycle Sequencing
(example, N=98)

Reagent	Volume per Sample	Total
ddH$_2$O	6.5μL*	637μL
BetterBuffer	5.0μL	490μL
BigDye Terminator v.1.1	1.0μL	98μL
Primer (3.3μM)	1.5μL	147μL

* volume of water required for cycle sequencing 1μL of PCR product; the volume of ddH$_2$O can be adjusted.

4. **In Hood**: Combine all master mix components in the order listed above into a labeled tube.

Y:\R&D Staff\Nicole\Active SOPs (word)\Active SOPs (Word)\Post PCR mtDNA Processing.Rev 1.doc
Created on 01/24/2009
Revised on 05/20/2009   Page 3 of 6   Approved: _____ 05/2009

mtDNA Sequence Analysis

Purpose: To analyze mitochondrial sequence data using Sequence Scanner v1.0 and Sequencher™ software. Sequence Scanner v1.0 is used to screen data quality and assess samples for reinjection and retesting. Sequencher™ is used for sequence analysis once samples have sequence verified in two directions or from separate amplifications for HV1 and HV2 of the mitochondrial genome.

Equipment and Supplies

- Sequence Scanner v1.0 (Applied Biosystems)
- Sequencher™ 4.7 or greater (Gene Codes Corporation)

Procedure

A. Assess Data Quality

Review sequence files using Sequence Scanner v1.0 immediately following electrophoresis on the ABI PRISM 3130*xl* Genetic Analyzer.

Note: The *Quality Metrics* scores are primer dependent and must be established prior to analysis. Refer to Appendix A for guidance.

1. Import .ab1 files into Sequence Scanner v1.0 to evaluate the quality of the sequences. Launch Sequence Scanner v1.0 software. Under the **File Tasks** menu, select [Import Traces]. Select the run folder(s) to analyze. To select multiple folders, hold Ctrl and click each folder using the mouse. Click **Add Selected Traces >>.** The traces are added to the column on the right. If these are the correct trace files, select **OK**.

2. Under the **Reports** menu, select [Show Reports]. Under the View Reports menu, select [Plate Report]. Review the Plate Report to assess the quality of data generated for the batch plate (Figure 1). Sample names can be added to the thumbnails by entering the **Edit** menu and selecting **Preferences**. Under the **Reports** menu tree, select **Plate Report**. Select **Show a smaller thumbnail and show the file name** for the **Settings for the Plate Report**. If the thumbnail border is grey, no amplified DNA was detected in the sequencing analysis (*e.g.*, Figure 1, well A1). Confirm that all ladder wells, negative controls, and reagent blanks have a grey thumbnail. Confirm green quality score for the positive control. If one of the controls fails, inform a supervisor to determine corrective action. If the thumbnail image displays an aberrant electropherogram in a well, a re-injection of that sample should be performed (regardless of quality score color).

Figure 1. Plate Report

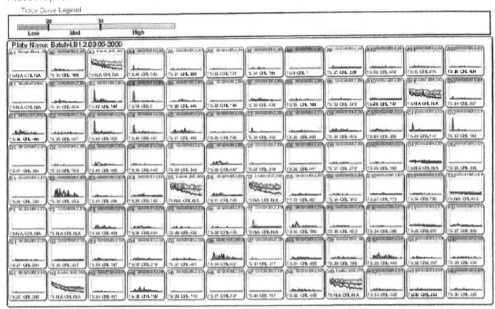

3. Under the **Reports** menu, select [Show Reports]. Under the View Reports menu, select [QC Report]. Print the Quality Control Report by selecting **File → Print**. The sequence data for each sample is color-coded for Trace Score and CRL. If the Trace Score and CRL are both green, the sequence passes the first filter and can be used for sequence analysis. If the Trace Score and CRL are both red, the sequence fails the first filter and must be retested; any sample may be viewed at the discretion of the analyst. All other color combinations are manually reviewed to assess the sequence quality (*e.g.*, yellow/red, yellow/green, yellow/yellow, etc.) (Table 1).

Table 1. Data Review using the Quality Control Report

Trace Score	CRL	Action
G	G	No review- sequence passed
G or Y	R or Y	Review
R or Y	G or Y	Review
R	R	No review- sequence failed

4. Launch the Trace file name in the Quality Control Report by clicking on sample name. Evaluate the raw and analyzed data for all samples flagged for review and document all reviews in the **Comments** column of the Quality Control Report. Suggested comments include, but are not limited to, the following: ✓, re-inject, low signal, no signal, C-stretch, partial sequence. Retain printout and comments for case file.

5. Perform necessary re-injections immediately, as samples can only be re-injected up to 48 hours at room temperature after XTerminator cleanup.

    Note: XTerminator products can be stored for up to 10 days at 4°C.

6. Check all acceptable sequences in the **Sequence Status Worksheet**.

B. First Read: Create the Sequencher Projects

Note: If this is the first time performing analysis on a particular computer, create a template that contains the revised Cambridge Reference Sequence. See Appendix B for guidance.

1. Import the files for analysis by selecting **File→Import→Sequences...** Select only the sample files that were determined to have acceptable sequence data. Under **Files of type:** select **With Chromatogram Sequences** from the pull-down menu. Click **Open** to import the highlighted sequences (Figure 2).

Figure 2. Import Sequences

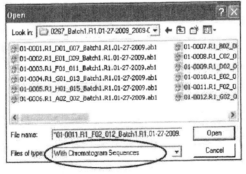

2. Trim poor quality data from the sequences using automatic trimming. In the menu bar, select **Sequence→Trim Ends...** In the Ends Trimming window, select **Trim Checked Items** and select **Trim**. Close the Ends Trimming window.

Note: If this is the first time analysis is being performed on a particular computer, the *Trim Criteria* need to be established. Refer to Appendix C for guidance.

Note: The trimmed data are fully recoverable because Sequencher retains both the original sequence and the edited copy. To recover the original sequence data, select **Sequence → Revert to Experimental Data.**

3. Once the acceptable sequence data have been imported and trimmed for all sequencing primers in a batch, highlight the sequences to be placed in a contig as well as the D-LOOP reference sequence 𝔦🔳 D-LOOP . Select **AbN,** then **Assembly Parameters.** Ensure that the *Assemble By Name* box at the bottom is checked to **Enabled** and then click **Name Settings…** Select the appropriate Name Delimiter from the drop-down menu as well as the appropriate handle. A name delimiter is defined as a character such as a hyphen or period which separates elements of a sequence name and a handle is defined as the portion of a sequence name between two consecutive delimiters. (Currently, the delimiter is a period for handle one). Select **OK.** Assemble sequences **To Reference by Name.** Confirm the *Expected Contigs* in the Assembly Preview window and select **Assemble.** A window will open indicating *Assembly Completed.* Close the window.

Note: If the software did not properly compile the files into a contig, highlight the contig(s) and select **Sequence→Dissolve Contig.** Return to the **Name Setting** menu, and alter the Name Delimiter and/or the handle until it is correct.

4. Click **File → Save Project.** In the *File name:* field, enter **Batch X.a,** where X represents the batch number and *.a* represents the first analyst's data analyses.

5. Click **File → Save Project As…** In the *File name:* field, enter **Batch X.b,** where X represents the batch number and *.b* represents the second analyst's data analyses.

6. Click **File → Save Project As…** In the *File name:* field, enter **Batch X.ALL,** where X represents the batch number. This project contains all sequence trace files used for analysis without modification/review.

C. Quality Control Checks

Note: This process can be performed by any analyst, but is typically performed by the first analyst.

1. Click **File → Open.** Select the *Batch X.a* project.

2. Confirm that all controls produce the expected results.

UNT Center for Human Identification
Procedure Manual – Research & Development Laboratory

a. Select the contig for the positive control HL60. Evaluate the sequence and export the Variance Report to the appropriate folder.

b. Open the Excel spreadsheet located at **Y:\R&D Worksheets\QC Worksheet.mtDNA Analysis** (project specific versions may be saved elsewhere). Enter the project name (if applicable) and complete the gray shaded fields in the top section.

c. Click in the cell indicated by the *Import text file here* → prompt (cell B10). Select **Data → Get External Data→ From Text**. Navigate to the location of the saved HL60 variance report. Select the file and click **Import**.

d. The *Text Import Wizard* will launch. Click **Finish**.

e. The *Import Data* dialog box will appear. Click **Properties…**, and deselect the box titled **Adjust column width.** Click **OK**. Verify that the specified cell for import says "B10". Click **OK**.

f. If the HL60 profile is concordant with the reference profile, "Yes" should appear in the boxes of the Concordant? column. See Figure 3 for the HL60 reference profile.

Figure 3. HL60 Expected Haplotype

Compare Consensus to Reference		HL60...	Total
Reference			
16,069	C	T	1
16,193	C	T	1
16,278	C	T	1
16,362	T	C	1
73	A	G	1
150	C	T	1
152	T	C	1
263	A	G	1
295	C	T	1
315.1	:	C	1
489	T	C	1
♦	Total	11	11

g. Inspect the negative control and reagent blank electropherograms. No interpretable sequence should be present. If the controls pass, select "pass" in the cells of the lower section.

Note: If any of the controls are not concordant with expected results, the analyst will investigate the cause and file a corrective action report. Any interpretable sequence in the negative control or reagent blank will be entered in the "*mito QA Database*" Specimen Category in the local database of LISA if the source is not identified. If the negative control and/or reagent blank produce interpretable sequence, the analyst will document the findings on the Corrective Action form and the supervisor will review and initial.

D. First Read: mtDNA Sequence Analysis

1. Click **File → Open.** Select the *Batch X.a* project.

2. Double-click on the contig for each sample to open (Figure 4).

Figure 4. Contig Overview

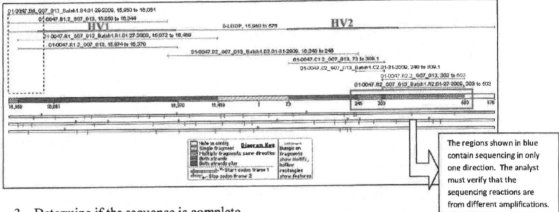

The regions shown in blue contain sequencing in only one direction. The analyst must verify that the sequencing reactions are from different amplifications.

3. Determine if the sequence is complete.
   - If HV1 and HV2 are not fully covered, document the samples to be reprocessed on **Cherry Picking Worksheet.**
   - If full coverage is obtained, refer to **Section G. Sequence Data Interpretation and Reporting** for the analysis and reporting procedures. Designate the sample as complete by checking the sample in the 1st **Read Complete** column of the **mtDNA Sequence Quality Checklist.**

4. Repeat Steps 2 and 3 for all contigs in the project.

5. Save changes to the *Batch X.a* project prior to exiting the software.

E. Second Read: mtDNA Sequence Analysis

1. Open the mtDNA Sequence Quality Checklist. Note which samples have check marks in the pink column titled *1st Review* and no check mark in the column titled *2nd Review*. These samples are ready for the second read.

2. Click **File → Open.** Select the *Batch X.b* project that contains the noted samples.

3. Refer to **Section G. Sequence Data Interpretation and Reporting** to analyze the complete sequence contigs and produce the appropriate reports for each sample.

4. Save changes to the *Batch X.b* project prior to exiting the software.

F. Second Read: Verify Concordance Between First and Second Reads

1. Open the first read project, titled *Batch X.a.*

2. **Ctrl+select** all of the sample contigs that have been reviewed by two analysts (*i.e.*, first and second reads complete). Click **File→ Export→Selection As Subproject**. Save the subproject in the batch folder named *Batch X Sequence Analysis → Sequencher Projects→Sequencer Subprojects*.

3. Open the *Batch X.b* project. Select **File → Save Project As...** In the *File name:* field, enter **Batch X.CC.1**, where *X* represents the batch number. Subsequent cherry picking concordance check projects should be saved with an extension of *.2, .3*, etc. as to not overwrite previous concordance checks.

4. **Ctrl+select** a pair of samples (seen in duplicate) that have been analyzed by two independent reviewers. Select **Contig →Validate mtDNA Profiles**. Click **Create Report →Save**. Navigate to the **Batch X Sequence Analysis → Concordance Check Reports** folder. In the *File name:* field, enter **XX-XXXX.CC**, where *XX-XXXX* represents the sample identification number. Click **Save**.

5. Repeat Step 4 for all of the samples in the project that have been second read.

6. Save changes to the *Batch X.CC* project prior to exiting.

7. Navigate to the Concordance Check Reports folder and **Ctrl+select** the reports that were exported. Right-click the selection and click **Print**.

8. Consult with the first reader to resolve any discrepancies and finalize the concordance report. Handwrite the following information on the concordance report: (1) the most conservative consensus range between the two analysts; and, (2) any confirmed length heteroplasmy. Both analysts' signatures are required on the finalized concordance report.

G.   Sequence Data Interpretation and Reporting

1. Double-click the sample contig; click **Bases→Show Chromatograms**. Confirm **each base** by at least two clean lanes of data (either from the forward and reverse sequences or from two separate amplifications). The analyst may refer to AFDIL Research Sequencing Calling Guide for Control Region (16024-576) for most conventional call of common mtDNA differences. Any ambiguity will be denoted as **N**. Point heteroplasmy will be designated according to International Union of Pure and Applied Chemistry (IUPAC) nomenclature for mtDNA variants:

Common:	Rare:
C/T = Y	G/T = K
A/G = R	T/A = W
	C/G = S
	A/C = M

Note: Up to four ambiguous base positions, or **Ns**, are acceptable for HV1 and HV2 combined. Data with greater than four ambiguities require additional sequencing.

Note: No IUPAC codes for a mixture of three bases (*e.g.*, B, D, or H) will be reported.

Note: Sequence data generated with the R1 primer exhibit reproducible artifacts from positions 16027-16039, with the majority of the noise from position 16030-16036. If the quality of the sequence using the B4 and/or B1 primer is good, this region of sequence is reported. The following figures provide examples of the artifacts seen in the R1 sequence data.

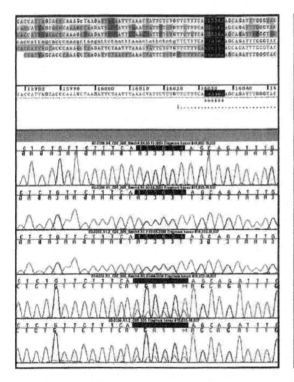
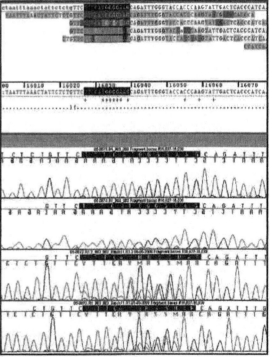

Note: Sequence data will be collected for as much of the Control Region as is reliable. Confirmed sequence obtained for complete HV1 (16024-16365) and HV2 (73-340) regions is considered "full sequence" for analysis and databasing purposes. If a contig needs to be reamplified or re-cycle sequenced, the first reader will note the primer(s) required in the Y:\DATA\Chile Database\Cherry Picking form under the *mito* tab. If the contig has complete coverage, the first reader will mark the sample as complete on the mtDNA Sequence Quality Checklist.

2. Once all base calls and edits are made for a contig, select **Contig→Compare Consensus to Reference**. Double-click on each base variant and verify the correct assignment in the electropherogram.

   Note: Verify that the software is set to report consensus sequence by plurality; select **Contig→Consensus By Plurality.**

3. Archive an electronic version of the reports in the *Variance Reports* folder for the appropriate batch on the Y:\ drive. Select *Variance Table Report* from the dropdown menu, and click **Save as Text**. In the *File name:* field, enter **XX-XXXX.INT**, where *XX-XXXX* is the sample identification number and *INT* is the analyst's initials. Navigate to the desired save location and click **Save**.

4. Navigate to the location of the saved variance reports. Open each variance report and manually enter the confirmed range(s) for analysis. Confirmed ranges can be determined by selecting **Contig → Consensus to Forensic Standards**. Also, report any length heteroplasmy at the bottom of the report using the following notation:

   location: major; minor; second minor *(when applicable);* see Figure 5 .

   Save changes to each variance report once complete.

Figure 5. Reporting Length Heteroplasmies

   Example: 303: C9TC6; C10TC6; C8TC6

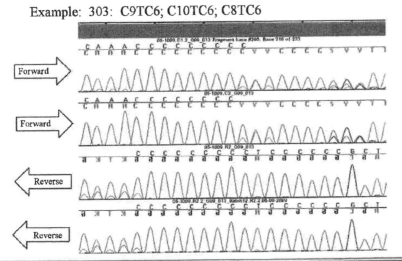

5. Select all of the variance reports for the batch with your initials (**Ctrl+select** for multiple files). Right-click the selection and select **Print**.

6. Initial each variance report by the date.

H. Repeat Analysis

Those results that do not meet minimum calling criteria will be repeated. The analyst will determine and document the best course of action (*e.g.*, re-extraction, re-amplification, re-cycle sequencing, etc.). Any additional sequence generated will be imported into all three projects: *Batch X.a*, *Batch X.b*, and *Batch X.ALL*. Quality control checks, first reads, second reads and concordance checks will be performed on the additional, complete samples as specified in Sections B-G of this protocol.

Controls: Upon repeat analysis, multiple primers may be retested on the same plate. Controls must be considered and appropriately applied with repeat analysis. Since all controls produced appropriate results in the initial testing, only a subset of controls is required for repeat analysis.

Re-extraction: A new reagent blank will be generated.

Re-amplification: A new positive and negative control will be generated. If amplification parameters are not altered from those in the previous amplification, the reagent blank does not need to be repeated. If amplification parameters are modified or additional template is added to the amplification (*e.g.*, increased template from 1 μL to 3 μL), then the reagent blank and the negative control must be repeated with the maximum volume added for any sample on the plate.

Re-cycle sequencing: If cycle sequencing parameters are not altered from those in the previous reactions, repeat the positive control only. It is not necessary to repeat the reagent blank or negative control. It is acceptable to perform cycle sequencing reactions on the same plate with multiple primers from multiple plates. The analyst must select controls following these criteria: (1) if different primers are being repeated for any sample from a plate, the positive control must be repeated for only one primer (it is recommended to use the primer most represented on the plate); (2) if a different volume of PCR product is added to the cycle sequencing reaction for a specific primer (*e.g.*, using 3μl of amplified product), the reagent blank and negative control must also be repeated with the maximum volume represented from that plate.

Note: If running one plate with several PCR plates represented, all three controls from each plate need to be re-cycle sequenced.

Note: If a positive control fails, the samples associated with that PCR plate will not be used for analysis.

Appendix A

Establishing the Quality Metrics Score Thresholds and Settings

Under the **Edit** menu, select **Preferences**. Under the **Traces** menu tree, select **Quality Metrics**. Set the **Trace Score Color and Range** to 0-20 for low quality (red), 20-34 for medium quality (yellow), and 34-100 for high quality scores (green). Set the **Contiguous Read Length Color and Range** according to the primer used. Click **OK**.

Note: To change the color of the indicator to green, right click on blue portion of the Trace Score and CRL range bars and select green.

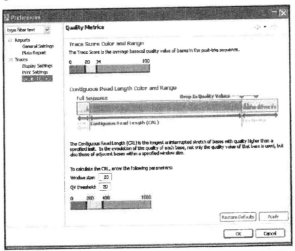

Note: Modify the CRL settings to account for shorter expected sequence reads. The CRL scores for B4 primer are set at 100 and 160, as shown below.

Appendix B

Importing the Revised Cambridge Reference Sequence

Launch the Sequencher™ software. Import the Revised Cambridge Reference Sequence by selecting **File→Import→ Sequencer Project...** The reference sequence is located at Y:\DATA\Chile Database. Select **D-LOOP.SPF** and select **Open**. Save the project as a template. Select **File→Save Project As Template...** Save project as *Template name:* **D-LOOP.**

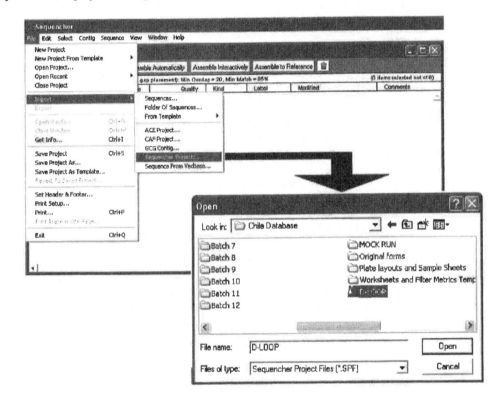

Appendix C
Establishing the Automatic Trimming Criteria

In the menu bar, select **Sequence→Trim Ends...** In the Ends Trimming window, select **Change Trim Criteria.** Select the settings displayed in the following figure. Click **OK.**

CPSIA information can be obtained
at www.ICGtesting.com
Printed in the USA
BVOW07s1030210316

441132BV00020B/487/P